Study Guide
Kim Dolgin
Ohio Wesleyan University

Child Development

Robert S. Feldman
University of Massachusetts - Amherst

PRENTICE HALL, *Upper Saddle River, NJ 07458*

© 1998 by PRENTICE-HALL, INC.
Simon & Schuster / A Viacom Company
Upper Saddle River, New Jersey 07458

ISBN 0-13-757642-0

Printed in the United States of America

TABLE OF CONTENTS

PREFACE

I've been teaching Child and Adolescent psychology for about fifteen years, and, frankly, I rarely recommend study guides to my students. Most of the study guides that I've seen are either too picky, too focused on vocabulary, or too arbitrary. Therefore, I was really pleased to be given the chance to write this study guide for Robert Feldman's text. Although I think he provides wonderful direction in each chapter about what you need to know, and presents the information clearly, in the study guide I have the opportunity to provide additional study aids.

While I was designing and writing it, I kept my own students in mind. What is always most important to me is that they get the main *concepts* down pat. Unfortunately, from a student's point of view, this often means learning some vocabulary at the same time. I've tried to design the study guide to help you do both more easily.

Each chapter is divided into several sections. All begin with a chapter outline and a set of real-life practical questions to spark your interest in the material. (What *is* the best parenting strategy? What determines whether a person is straight or gay?) There are page numbers with these questions in case you are really interested in the answers. Next follows a list of *Learning Objectives:* my distillation of the 15 to 20 most important concepts in the chapter. You can think of them as essay questions, and by the time you finish reviewing the text chapter and doing the study guide, you should be able to answer each without looking at your notes.

The *Guided Review* is next. This section, comprised of a text summary with blank spaces and an answer key on the right-hand side, walks you through the chapter's material pretty much in the order it is presented in the text. Cover up the answers and try reading the summary while filling in your own words. It will most likely take you a number of run-throughs, but once you can do it you should have most of the chapter's main points down.

In order to make vocabulary learning more interesting, I've put the key words found at the end of each text chapter, as well as other words that are italicized or highlighted in the text, into a *Crossword Puzzle.* The *Test Solutions* can be found at the end of each study guide chapter.

My favorite section is the *Flash Cards.* I always tell my students to make up flash cards, because I really think that using them is the very best way to study. Please cut them out and try them! Flash cards have a number of advantages. Most importantly, they require you to come up with the answer when you can't see it: reading your notes or your text over and over does not do this. I've found that oftentimes my students think they know the material because when they read their notes or their text it seems very familiar. Recognizing something when you're staring at it and being able to recall it when it's not there (like a test) are two entirely different things, however. Flash cards get around this problem. The flash cards I made up are mostly conceptual; if you're having trouble with the vocabulary words, I suggest you make up some more of your own with the word on one side and the definition on the back. A second advantage of flash cards is that they are easy to carry around in a backpack or purse. If you toss them in there, you can put them out whenever you have five or ten minutes to kill (like when you're waiting for a class to start or the dryer to finish). Many of my students think that "studying" must entail going to the library and sitting down for two hours. Not so! Studying in short bursts is a much better strategy, so carry around the flash cards and work on them in small bits when you have time. You can probably painlessly fit in half an hour per day without even feeling it. Finally, flash cards are good because you can continually cull the stack of them as you learn the material. In other words, if you've gotten a question right the last three times you went through the pile, put it aside and work only on those questions that are still giving you trouble. This is more efficient than rereading and rereading your entire page of notes, much of which you already know.

Finally, each chapter ends with a multiple choice ***Practice Test*** . There is one question for each of the initial Learning Objectives. Go back and review the material about that Objective if you find the question difficult.

That's it! Happy studying!

CHAPTER 1

An Introduction to Child Development

INTERESTING AND IMPORTANT THINGS YOU'LL KNOW AFTER READING THIS CHAPTER...

1. How long have doctors been making test-tube babies? See page 5.

2. Do children grow and change gradually or abruptly, in spurts? See page 12.

3. How can we work to stem the tide of growing youth violence? See page 15.

4. Are children really sexual beings? See page 18.

5. How has American family life changed since the 1800s? See page 34.

6. How safe is it for a child to participate in psychological research? See page 36.

Learning Objectives

When you have mastered the material in this chapter, you should be able to ...

1. Describe the field of child development, and be aware of its scope and range. (page 7)

2. List the 5 major life stages studied by child psychologists. (page 8)

3. Explain the ecological approach to child development, and understand how the different, nested levels of the environment can each affect a child. (page 9)

4. Understand the different types of forces that mold a child's development. (page 11)

5. Delineate the four major, over-arching issues of development that are studied by child psychologists. (page 12)

6. Describe Freud's psychodynamic perspective on personality structure and outline the stages of psychosexual personality development. (page 18)

7. Characterize Erikson's psychosocial personality theory. (page 19)

8. Explain the role of classical conditioning, operant conditioning, and social learning in development. (page 21)

9. Define the terms "assimilation" and "accommodation" and understand their role in cognitive development. (page 24)

10. Contrast the Piagetian and information-processing approaches to cognitive development. (page 25)

11. Discuss the role that cultural differences and ethnicity play in fostering development. (page 26)

12. Explain how child psychologists use theories, hypotheses, and the scientific method to learn about children. (page 29)

13. Contrast and understand the differences between experimental and correlational research. (page 30)

14. Evaluate the pros and cons of longitudinal, cross-sectional, and cross-sequential research designs. (page 33)

15. Describe the precautions taken by child psychologists to ensure subject safety when doing studies with children. (page 36)

Guided Review

Orientation to Child Development

The field of child _____ involves the _____ study of development. It studies individuals ranging in age from _____ through _____. Child psychologists study _____, _____, social, and _____ development.

development (5); scientific (6)

conception (6); adolescence (6)
cognitive; physical; personality (7)

It is important to remember that the _____ has important influences on development. The _____ approach emphasizes the role of _____ environmental layers. Things children encounter in their everyday lives make up the _____; its elements are linked in the _____. The _____ is composed of larger social institutions, while the _____ represents larger cultural values.

environment (9)
ecological (9)
four (9)

microsystem (9); mesosystem (9) exosystem (10)
macrosystem (10)

People in your _____ are others who were born at about the same time as you. They experienced the same normative _____ influences as you. In addition, you all experienced the normative _____ experiences of learning to walk and puberty at about the same time. Of course, your experiences differed from theirs due to your ethnicity, _____, and subcultural membership. Also, you each experienced unique _____ life events.

cohort (11)

history-graded (11)
age-graded (11)

socioeconomic status (12)

nonnormative (12)

Child development was established in the _____ century. Since that time, developmentalists have argued whether growth is gradual or _____ and about the import of critical, or as they are now conceptualized, _____ periods. There is constant debate as to whether it is better to take a _____ approach or to focus on a more specific period of development. Most importantly, child psychologists have tried to disentangle the contributions of _____, or maturation, and _____, or the environment.

late 18th (12)

discontinuous (12)

sensitive (13)
life span (13)

nature (14); nurture (14)

Theoretical Perspectives

Until fairly recently, children were viewed as _____ adults. This view has been supplanted by three major _____ of development.

miniature (17)

theories (18)

Freud (18); psychoanalytic (18)
unconscious (19)

id (19)
ego (19); superego (19)

five (19)
latency (19)

Erikson's (19); psychosexual (19)
life span (19)

men's (21)

predictions (21); future (21)

behavioral (21); observable (21) quantitative (21)
classical (21)

transferred (22); Operant (22)
voluntary (22)
weakened (22)
behavior modification (22)

Social (23)
Bandura (23)
dominate (23)

cognitive (23)
mind (23); Piaget (24);
schemes (24)

assimilation (24)
accommodation (24)

sequence (24)
earlier (24)
universal (24)

Information processing (25)
quantitative (25)

_____ was the founder of the _____ perspective of development, which emphasizes the role of the _____ in shaping behavior. He believed that the personality had three parts: the _____, which is filled with primitive drives, the _____, or rational part of the self, and the _____, or conscious self. He also believed that children move through _____ stages of psychosexual development as they mature: the oral, anal, phallic, _____, and genital stages.

Closely related is _____ theory of _____ development. Unlike Freud, Erikson believed that development continued through one's _____.

Both Freud's and Erikson's theories focused more on _____ behavior than on women's, and both lack the ability to make good _____ about _____ behavior.

The _____ perspective stresses learning and _____ behavior. Change is seen as _____. One type of learning, _____ conditioning, occurs when a neutral stimulus comes to take on meaning. This occurs because a response is _____ from one stimulus to another. _____ conditioning occurs when a _____ response is strengthened or _____ because of its consequences. These principles form the basis for _____, a set of techniques used to change people's behavior.

_____ learning, or observational learning, is equally important. Albert _____ is the most influential proponent of this type of learning, which has come to _____ the field in recent years.

The _____ perspective explicitly focuses upon the developing _____. _____, the founder of this perspective, believed that the mind contains _____ which represent actions. Children become smarter through the twin processes of _____ (understanding the world according to existing structures) and _____ (inventing new ways of thinking to cope with new experiences). Piaget's broad _____ of development is accurate, but some skills emerge _____ than he believed and some of his stages are not _____.

_____ is an alternative approach. This theory takes a more _____ view than Piaget's.

Research Methods

Child psychologists use the _____ method to study children; this involves the _____ collection of data. Data is used to formulate _____, broad descriptions of phenomena. Specific _____ are derived from them, and are useful because they can be _____.

scientific (29)
systematic (29)
theories (29)
hypotheses (29)
tested (29)

Experimental research is desirable because it lets psychologists discover _____ relationships among variables; _____ research only tells us whether a relationship between two factors exists.

causal (30)
correlational (30)

The people participating in an experiment are called _____. They are usually divided into treatment and _____ groups, who receive different forms of the _____ variable. The data collected is called the _____ variable.

subjects (30)
control (30)
independent (31); dependent (31)

Psychologists do correlational research because it can be _____ or _____ to conduct experiments. This kind of research cannot explain _____. Two types of correlational research are _____ and _____ research.

impossible (32); unethical (32)
causation (32)
case studies (33); survey (33)

Research, whether experimental or correlational, usually uses _____ of subjects. It can be conducted in the _____ or in the _____, in real-life settings. If this latter type of study is done, the researchers typically use _____ observation.

samples (33)
laboratory (33); field (33)

naturalistic (33)

There are three techniques used to measure developmental change. _____ research follows a group of individuals as they age. _____ research compares persons of different ages at the same time. It can be done _____, but can be plagued by _____ effects and cannot tell us about _____ in individuals. Some researchers combine these two techniques in _____ studies.

Longitudinal (34)
Cross-sectional (35)
quickly (35)
cohort (36)
changes (36)
cross-sequential (36)

All psychologists follow _____ guidelines which ensure their subjects' safety. These include freedom from _____, _____ consent, and maintenance of _____.

ethical (36)
harm (37)
informed (37); privacy (38)

Introduction to Child Development

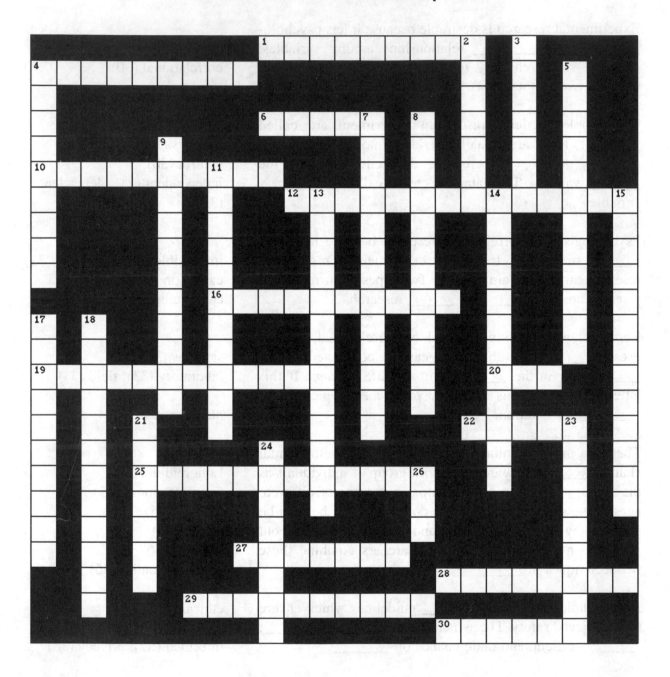

Across

1. _____ periods are times when one can easily acquire a new ability.
4. Only experiments can determine this.
6. The founder of the psychoanalytic perspective of personality development
10. Cross-_____ designs follow several groups of individuals over time.
12. The perspective that says people are motivated by unconscious forces
16. The perspective suggesting that different levels of the environment simultaneously influence individuals
19. According to Freud, the series of stages that children pass through as they mature
20. Normative ___-graded influences: e.g., learning to walk, reaching puberty
22. These studies are done in "real life" settings.
25. Idiosyncratic, unique events
27. Normative _____-graded influences: e.g., being raised during a period of famine
28. A synonym for your conscience
29. The approach that emphasizes the role of the environment in shaping behavior
30. A group of people born at about the same time in the same place

Down

2. The founder of the psychosocial perspective of development
3. The group in an experiment that does not receive the experimental treatment
4. The type of conditioning in which a neutral stimulus comes to take on meaning
5. These studies follow one group of individuals over a protracted period of time.
7. Changing quickly in spurts
8. The Piagetian form of learning that involves changing the way you view the world due to a new experience
9. _____ processors study memory, attention, and problem-solving.
11. The variable manipulated by the experimenter
13. Normative _____-graded influences: e.g., being an Asian-American female
14. A form of Piagetian learning in which you acquire new knowledge but do not build any new schemata
15. These studies examine the relationship between pre-existing groups.
17. A type of study in which a researcher devises two or more treatments for different groups of subjects
18. Erikson's branch of psychology
21. The last of Freud's psychosexual stages
23. _____ variable: the data collected in an experiment
24. _____ period: the only point in development at which you can acquire an ability
26. The rational part of the self

Flash Cards

What are the four main types of development studied by psychologists?

List the five main stages of development studied by child and adolescent psychologists.

What are the four nesting layers of the environment discussed by ecological psychologists?

Give an example of something that is a part of a child's microsystem.

Give an example of something that is part of a child's macrosystem.

In what way is American society individualistic, as opposed to collectivistic?

Give several examples of normative history-graded influences on development.

Give several examples of normative age-graded influences on development.

Give several examples of nonnormative life events that can affect development.

Contrast continuous and discontinuous perceptions of developmental change.

The prenatal period (conception through birth), infancy and toddlerhood (birth to 3 years), the preschool period (3 to 6 years), middle childhood (6 to 12 years), and adolescence (12 to 20)	Social development, cognitive development, physical development, and personality development
His or her parents, day care workers, brothers and sisters, their home	The microsystem, the mesosystem, the exosystem, and the macrosystem
American society values personal achievement, individual identity, freedom, and individual worth.	Societal values, one's religion, one's country's political system
Everyone learns to walk and speak and hits puberty at approximately the same age.	People born during the Great Depression or who were of draftable age during World War II were greatly influenced by these events.
Continuous development holds that children change gradually, a little every day; discontinuous development is development in abruptly changing stages.	A person is left crippled after a car accident at age 6; another's father dies when she is 11; another moves to a different country for a period of 2 years during middle school.

Contrast the terms "critical period" and "sensitive period". Which is the more modern conception?

Name several traits that are indisputably produced by "nature."

Name several traits that are indisputably largely influenced by "nurture."

Give an example of how nature and nurture mutually influence each other.

Describe the id.

List Freud's five stages of psychosexual development.

According to Freud, why do adults develop fixations?

How does Erikson's theory differ from Freud's?

Critique Freud's psychodynamic theory.

What developmental perspective was championed by John Watson?

Describe B. F. Skinner's contributions to psychology.

What are the four steps in the social learning process?

One's eye color and hair color; one's blood type; whether one can see in color

If some trait can develop *only* at a certain time of life, that is a critical period; if it is more easily acquired then, we call it a sensitive period. Sensitive period is currently more favored.

If a baby cries frequently, his parents will stop running to him quickly each time he cries. Thus, his temperament has influenced his environment.

One's taste in music or food; the clothes one chooses to wear; one's favorite color

(1) Oral stage, birth - 1 year;
(2) anal stage, 1-3 years;
(3) phallic stage, 3-6 years;
(4) latency, 6-12 years;
(5) genital stage, 12 years on

The id is largely in the unconscious. It operates on the pleasure principle, and is the seat of sexual and aggressive urges. It is present from birth.

Erikson's theory is different in that it takes a lifespan perspective. Freud believed that personality development was complete by age 12.

Fixations develop because of unresolved conflicts during earlier developmental stages.

The behavioral approach. Watson believed that children were infinitely malleable.

Although most psychologists believe in the unconscious, there is little data in support of most of the rest of Freud's theory.

(1) Observer must pay attention;
(2) must recall behavior;
(3) must be able to perform behavior
(4) must be motivated to perform it

Skinner "invented" operant conditioning, and proved the importance of reinforcement and punishment on behavior.

Who has had the greatest impact on the field of cognitive development?

What are *schemes?*

Give an example of accommodation.

Give three criticisms of Piaget's work.

Contrast the terms "race" and "ethnicity."

What is the relationship between theories and hypotheses?

Child psychology is considered a science. What does that mean?

Why are experiments better than other forms of research?

Why might a researcher engage in correlational research?

Describe two types of correlational research.

What are the advantages of a lab study over a field study?

What is one advantage of longitudinal research?

Organized mental patterns that represent behaviors and actions.	Jean Piaget
1. Some skills emerge earlier than he believed. 2. His stages are not universal. 3. Development is more continuous than he suggested.	I have always liked cats. I think they're nice. I bend down to scratch my neighbor's cat and she scratches me. I decide that not all cats are nice.
Theories are broad explanations of a phenomenon. Hypotheses are specific, testable issues generated from theories.	Race is a biological construct. Ethnicity is a term used to describe the patterns of a person's behaviors and sense of identity.
Only experiments can answer questions about causality.	It means that psychologists learn about children by making careful, systematic observations.
Case studies (intensive examination of one or a few persons) and surveys (in which you question large numbers of persons)	It is not always ethical or possible to engage in experimental research, e.g., you would never hit someone's head so that you could study brain damage.
Longitudinal research lets you see how individuals change — or remain the same — over time.	The researcher has more control over events in the lab, and can make sure that the situation faced by subjects is constant.

What are the two most recent changes in American family life?	What are some disadvantages of longitudinal research?
What are the two main disadvantages of cross-sectional research?	Describe the cross-sequential research design.
What are three ethical guidelines that must be followed when conducting psychological research?	How does social learning differ from both classical and operant conditioning?

(1) That subjects become "test-wise" over time;
(2) that subjects drop out of the study;
(3) they take a long time to complete

(1) That most mothers now work full-time outside the home;
(2) that there is an increase in the number of single-parent, female-headed families

You begin with several age groups (like a cross-sectional study) and then track these groups over time (like a longitudinal study).

(1) They don't control for cohort affects;
(2) they can't track individual differences over time

It places more emphasis upon the inner workings of the mind, and looks less to the consequences of behavior.

Psychologists must protect their subjects' privacy, must ensure them freedom from harm, and must obtain informed consent.

Practice Test One

1. A psychologist interested in the study of cognitive development would most likely study
   a. a child's shyness.
   b. the ability to crawl.
   c. memory development.
   d. nonverbal communication.

2. _____ lasts from about age 6 to age 12.
   a. Middle childhood
   b. Early childhood
   c. Toddlerhood
   d. Adolescence

3. Which of the following would be in the exosystem?
   a. the child's sitter's home
   b. the mother's workplace
   c. the political values of the child's society
   d. the local government

4. An example of a nonnormative life event would be
   a. being born during a famine.
   b. learning to crawl at six months.
   c. a parent's injury in a serious car accident.
   d. being an Asian American female.

5. A person who believes that most human behavior is inborn and caused by a person's genetic make-up believes in
   a. development.
   b. nurture.
   c. development.
   d. nature.

6. The genital stage of personality development begins
   a. at birth.
   b. at 1 year of age.
   c. at 6 years of age.
   d. at 12 years of age.

7. Erikson believed that we move through _____ stages of development.
   a. 4
   b. 5
   c. 6
   d. 8

8. Shelly has started smoking even though her mother, who also smokes, strongly disapproves of her behavior. This is an example of
   a. classical conditioning.
   b. social learning.
   c. operant conditioning.
   d. assimilation.

9. Thomas has decided that math, which he had always enjoyed, is "yucky" ever since he was required to learn geometry. This is an example of
   a. accommodation.
   b. classical conditioning.
   c. social learning.
   d. assimilation.

10. Which of the following statements is correct?
    a. Piagetians and information processors both believe that development is continuous.
    b. Piagetians and information processors both believe that development is discontinuous.
    c. Piagetians view development as continuous, while information processors see it as discontinuous.
    d. Piagetians view development as discontinuous, while information processors see it as continuous.

11. American society is
    a. collectivistic.   c. pre-emptory.
    b. individualistic.   d. theocratic.

12. Dr. Marston is conducting an experiment in which he is giving one group of children violin lessons and a second group art lessons. At the end of the experiment, he plans to see if one group has developed better fine motor control than the other. The independent variable in this study is
    a. the type of lessons received.
    b. the children's performance on a test of fine motor skills.
    c. the children.
    d. the belief that lessons might improve fine motor skill.

13. Tim's pediatrician just completed a study which examined several of the factors that seem to influence children's weight. One of these factors was the child's participation in team sports. Tim's weight was compiled with the group of children who do participate in team sports, since he is on a soccer team. This is an example of
    a. a true experiment.
    b. a correlational study.
    c. either (a) or (b), you cannot determine from the given information.
    d. neither (a) nor (b).

14. Which of the following can tell you about the stability of an individual's traits over time?
    a. only cross-sequential research   c. only cross-sectional research
    b. only longitudinal research   d. both (a) and (b)

15. When Dr. Freeman puts only a number code on Francis' data sheet, he is
    a. ensuring Francis' privacy.
    b. protecting Francis from harm.
    c. deceiving Francis.
    d. collecting informed consent.

Test Solutions

Self-Quiz Solution

1. c (page 7)
2. a (page 8)
3. d (page 10)
4. a (page 11)
5. d (page 14)
6. d (page 20)
7. d (page 19)
8. b (page 23)

9. a (page 24)
10. d (page 25)
11. b (page 27)
12. a (page 31)
13. b (page 32)
14. d (page 34)
15. a (page 38)

Crossword Puzzle Solution

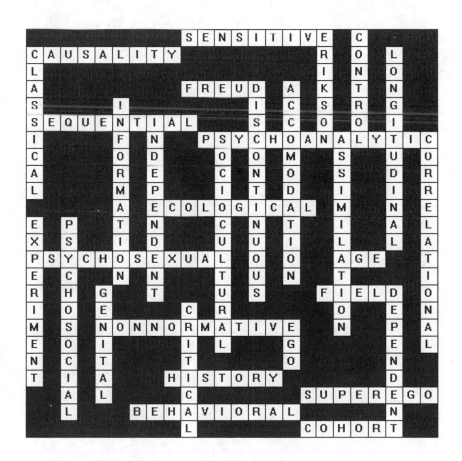

CHAPTER 2

The Start of Life: Prenatal Development

INTERESTING AND IMPORTANT THINGS YOU'LL KNOW AFTER READING THIS CHAPTER...

1. Why are some twins identical while others are not? See page 48.

2. How can two parents who have the same trait — like dark brown hair — have a child with a different trait — like red hair? See page 50.

3. Why can it be beneficial to have a certain, painful type of anemia? See page 54.

4. What are some of the ways that doctors and genetic counselors can determine whether an unborn child is likely to develop any genetic disorders? See page 56.

5. How do some of the new treatments used to help infertile couples have children work? See page 59.

6. How much influence do your genes have over your intelligence? See page 63. Your personality? See page 64.

7. When is a fetus first capable of moving and reacting to stimulation? See page 72.

8. Which drugs should pregnant women avoid? See pages 75-77.

Learning Objectives

When you have mastered the material in this chapter, you should be able to ...

1. Understand the differences between sperm and ova. (46)

2. Describe how genetic information is carried in our cells, and how this information makes us male or female. (47)

3. Explain how genes work in combination to shape our traits. (50)

4. Describe the symptoms of several important genetic disorders. (54)

5. Compare and contrast the most common forms of prenatal testing. (56)

6. Describe several techniques available to help infertile couples. (59)

7. Understand how researchers study the relative effects of genes and environment in shaping a person's traits. (62)

8. Describe the degree to which heredity and environment influence our intelligence and personality. (63)

9. Contrast the three different types of gene-environment interactions. (69)

10. Characterize the three stages of prenatal development. (72)

11. Understand how the mother's diet, age, health, and habits can affect prenatal development. (73)

12. Describe how fathers can affect their child's prenatal development. (77)

13. Explain positive steps that pregnant women can take to ensure that their baby will develop properly during the prenatal period. (77)

Guided Review

Heredity

Prenatal development begins when two _____, or sex cells, fuse to form a _____. Usually a single _____ matures in a woman's body each month; in contrast, men produce several hundred _____ _____ per day.

gametes (46)
zygote (46); egg (47)

million (47); sperm (47)

_____, the basic units of genetic information, are composed of _____. They are arranged in 46 chains called _____. Because of _____, tens of trillions of combinations are possible. Therefore, only _____ twins share identical genes. Females have _____ chromosomes; males have one _____ and one _____ chromosome.

Genes (47)
DNA (47)
chromosomes (47); meiosis (48); monozygotic (48)
two X (49)
X (49); Y (49)

Sometimes genes are not of equal strength. _____ genes are expressed when they are paired with _____ genes. People who have two identical copies of a gene are called _____, while people with two different copies are termed _____. Since environment often contributes to a trait, one's _____ is often different from one's _____. Sometimes one pair of genes controls a trait, such as in PKU, or _____; sometimes traits are _____.

Dominant (50)
recessive (50)

homozygous (51)
heterozygous (51)
phenotype (51); genotype (51)

phenylketonuria (51); polygenic (53)

Fortunately, _____ can now sometimes tell, before a child is born, whether it has certain harmful conditions. _____ involve withdrawing a sample of the fluid surrounding the fetus. _____ sampling involves taking a sample of the tissue that surrounds the fetus. Less invasive, _____ allows doctors to see a televised image of the fetus.

genetic counselors (56)

Amniocenteses (56)
Chorionic villus (56)

ultrasound (56)

About _____ of couples suffer from _____. _____ fertilization occurs on a petri dish; the zygote can then be implanted in the woman who provided the egg or in a _____.

15% ; infertility (59); In vitro (59)

surrogate (59)

The Interaction of Heredity and Environment

Heredity, or _____, and environment, or _____, interact to produce a person's traits.

nature (61) nurture (61)

breed (62)

generalizing (62)
monozygotic (62)

unrelated (62)
environment (62)

adopted (63); birth (63)

do (63)
increase (63); 50 to 70 (64)

Neuroticism; (64) extroversion
(65)
risk-taking; (65); traditionalism
(65)
philosophies (66)

schizophrenia (68); autism
(69); alcoholism (69)

active gene-environment (69)

passive gene-environment (69)

evocative gene-environment
(69)

three (70)
germinal (70); conception
2 weeks (70); rapidly (71)
specialized (71)

One way researchers study the effects of heredity and environment is to selectively _____ animals so that their genes are different. This technique is useful even though we must be cautious about _____ these findings to humans. Humans can be directly studied. Comparisons of _____ twins allow us to compare individuals with identical genetic endowments; studying _____ children reared together lets us examine the role of the _____ in shaping behavior. We can also compare the relative similarities of children with their _____ and _____ parents.

Genetics _____ play a significant role in intelligence, and genes' role seems to _____ with age. About _____ percent of intelligence can be accounted for by genetics.

_____, or moodiness and sensitivity, as well as _____, or outgoingness, are two personality traits with a significant genetic component. So are _____ and _____. Kagen has even suggested that differences in heredity predispose different cultures to different _____.

Several psychological disorders, such as _____, _____, and _____ are certainly under partial genetic control.

Genes and environment interact in different ways. For example, a solitary child may like to read while an outgoing child may choose to join the drama club; this is an _____ interaction. Conversely, a child may be given no say as to which 3rd grade homeroom teacher he may have; this is a _____ interaction. Finally, a fearful child might cause his father to keep him closer to home than he might otherwise do; this is an example of an _____ interaction.

Prenatal Growth and Change

There are _____ stages of prenatal development. The first, the _____ stage, begins with _____ and lasts for _____. During this stage, cells divide _____ and become increasingly _____.

By the beginning of the second, _____ stage, the zygote — now called an _____ — is attached to the uterine wall. At first the _____ has _____ layers. The _____ will become skin and sense organs. The mesoderm will form _____, bones, and _____. The _____ will produce the respiratory and _____ systems as well as the _____.

embryonic (71)
embryo (71)
embryo; 3 (72)
ectoderm (72)
muscle (72); circulatory organs (72); endoderm (72); digestive (72); liver (7)

The third stage, the _____ stage, begins at the end of the _____ week of prenatal development and lasts until _____. The fetus _____ rapidly. By about 4 months post-conception the mother can feel the fetus _____.

fetal (72)
8th (72)
birth (72); grows (72)
move (72)

A _____ is a factor that produces birth defects. To help ensure a healthy baby, mothers should eat a _____ diet. Women older than 30 are at increased risk of having babies who are born _____ or who have _____. Adolescent mothers are also at risk for _____ births.

teratogen (73)
balanced (73)

prematurely (74); Down's syndrome (75); premature (75)

Maternal illness can hinder prenatal development. In particular, _____ can cause blindness, deafness and _____ defects, while _____ increases the risk of _____. A relatively recent and deadly concern is _____: a full _____ of babies whose mothers are affected contract the virus. These babies rarely live past _____.

rubella (75); heart (75);
mumps (75); miscarriage (75)
AIDS (75)
30% (75)
infancy (75)

Pregnant women should avoid unnecessary _____ use. Even "harmless" _____ can cause fetal bleeding. _____, a drug formerly used to prevent _____, causes particularly severe symptoms. Both marijuana and _____ restrict a fetus' oxygen supply. _____ syndrome, a condition leading to mental retardation and _____ deformities, occurs when pregnant women ingest too much alcohol. Even fetuses whose mothers have as few as _____ drinks per day are at increased risk.

drug (75)
aspirin (75)
Thalidomide (75); morning sickness (75)
cocaine (76); Fetal alcohol (77)

facial (77)

two (76)

_____, too, can affect their child's prenatal development. For example, fathers who _____ have children with lower _____.

Fathers (77)
smoke (77)
birth weights (77)

Precautions that women can take to optimize prenatal development include getting _____ to avoid harmful diseases, not _____ or _____, and continuing or beginning to _____.

vaccinations (78)
smoking (78); drinking alcohol (78); exercise (78)

Crossword Puzzle

The Start of Life: Prenatal Development

Across

3   _____ syndrome is a disorder produced by the presence of an additional 21st chromosome.

8   The pattern of emotional behavior present from birth.

11 _____ villus sampling is a prenatal test involving snipping off a piece of one of the fetal membranes.

18 The substance of which genes are composed

19 Traits that are determined by a combination of genes and environmental input

21 A factor that causes birth defects

22 A sex cell; a sperm or ovum

24 An individual's underlying genetic code

25 _____ genotype-environment interaction: when the child's genotype produces a particular environmental response

Down

1   The trait that is expressed when two competing traits are present

2   The second of the three stages of prenatal development

4   The stage of prenatal development that is approximately two weeks long

5   _____ genotype-environment interactions occur when children choose the alternatives in which they will participate

6   Fetal _____ syndrome can result in mental retardation and delayed growth.

7   Having inherited different forms of the same gene from one's parents

9   This type of twin is identical to his/her other twin.

10 _____ syndrome occurs when there is an extra X chromosome present.

12 The moment when sperm and ovum fuse.

13 A prenatal test in which a sample of the fluid that surrounds the fetus is withdrawn and analyzed

14 A prenatal test using high frequency sound waves

15 Rod-shaped portions of DNA containing many genes

16 _____ mothers are women who are paid to be artificially inseminated and carry a baby to term for an infertile couple.

17 Having a matching, identical pair of genes

20 The longest of the three prenatal stages

23 Another term for the fertilized egg

Flash Cards

Describe Nieman-Pick disease.	Contrast the terms "gamete" and "zygote."
How does mitosis differ from miosis?	How are dizygotic twins produced?
Who was Gregor Mandel?	What happens to a person who is *pp* for the PKU gene?
Why are genes on the X chromosome more likely to affect males?	What causes Down's syndrome?
Name a genetic disorder most likely to affect Jews of northern European descent.	What is the chromosomal complement of a person with Klinefelter's syndrome?

Gametes (sperm and egg) fuse during conception to form the zygote.

It is a fatal genetic disorder that causes slurred speech and imbalance.

Dizygotic twins result when two separate sperm fertilize two separate eggs.

Mitosis results in new cells with 46 chromosomes, whereas miosis results in cells with 23 chromosomes.

They fail to metabolize phenylalanine, and may become mentally retarded.

Mendel was an Austrian monk who discovered dominant and recessive traits.

An extra 21st chromosome.

Because they lack another X chromosome to counteract the effects of a gene on their X chromosome.

XXY

Tay-Sach's disease.

What is the advantage to having one gene for sickle-cell anemia?

Why are amniocenteses more common than chorionic villus sampling tests?

What causes infertility?

How can animal studies tell us about nature-nurture interaction?

How can monozygotic twins tell us about the effects of genes and environment?

How can dizygotic twins tell us about the effects of genes and environment?

How might a trait such as television watching be influenced by genetics?

What environmental factor seems to contribute to schizophrenia?

Contrast active and evocative gene-environment interactions.

Describe the appearance of an 8-week-old embryo.

List several behaviors that fetuses perform.

What is DES?

Because they are safer and can identify more problems.	People with only 1 sickle-cell gene are relatively healthy and protected from malaria.
Genetically different strains of animals can be bred. If these animals are raised in similar environments, any variation in their behavior must be genetic.	Age, prior use of birth control pills, smoking, low sperm counts, previous exposure to STD's
Similarities between pairs of dizygotic twins can be compared to similarities between pairs of monozygotic twins.	Monozygotic twins are genetically identical; any differences in their behavior must be caused by the environment.
Stress	People who like to watch television may be less social and physically active than persons who don't like to watch television; these traits are partially genetic.
One inch long, with a tail and gill slits. It has arm and leg buds, as well as rudimentary facial features.	In active interactions, children choose their own activity/environment; in evocative interactions, children elicit different responses from the same environment.
DES was a drug given to women through the 1970s to help prevent miscarriage. Fetuses exposed to DES have high cancer rates.	Fetuses turn, hiccup, open and close their fists, suck their thumbs, and hear.

What special problems do babies born to crack-addicted mothers have?	What happens to a fetus when its mother smokes?

Their blood oxygen levels drop
and their heart rate increases.

They are small, often addicted
themselves, have respiratory
problems, and are difficult
to soothe.

Practice Test One

1. Comparing eggs to sperm, eggs
   a. have a shorter life span.
   b. are more plentiful.
   c. are produced by both men and women.
   d. are less mobile.

2. Which statement best describes our chromosomes?
   a. Humans have 46 distinctly different types of chromosomes.
   b. There are no chromosomal differences between men and women.
   c. We have 23 pairs of chromosomes.
   d. Humans have over 100,000 chromosomes.

3. Gina's mother has blonde hair while her father has dark brown hair. Which of the following must be true?
   a. Gina is heterozygous for blonde hair.
   b. Gina's mother is heterozygous for blonde hair.
   c. Gina's father is heterozygous for dark brown hair.
   d. None of the above are true.

4. Martin has a severe case of sickle-cell anemia. Martin is probably
   a. African-American.
   b. Jewish.
   c. Italian.
   d. Asian.

5. Which of the following genetic tests can be performed before a woman becomes pregnant?
   a. ultrasound sonography
   b. amniocenteses
   c. chorionic villus sampling tests
   d. none of the above

6. Children who were conceived using "artificial" methods are
   a. generally as well adjusted as other children.
   b. usually frail and frequently ill.
   c. often put up for adoption.
   d. more likely to be abused than other children.

7. A limitation of using animals to study the effects of heredity and environment is
   a. that environment does not contribute to most animals' traits.
   b. that animals do not make good subjects.
   c. that it is often difficult to generalize the findings to humans.
   d. it is unethical to breed animals.

8. On average, environment contributes about _____to a person's intelligence.
   a. 10-30%
   b. 30-50%
   c. 50-70%
   d. 70-90%

9. Martin's parents wanted him to learn to speak French (even though he has little interest in the subject), and so they sent him to a school in which French is spoken during most of the day. This is an example of a(n)
   a. evocative gene-environment interaction.
   b. active gene-environment interaction.
   c. confounded gene-environment interaction.
   d. passive gene-environment interaction.

10. During the fetal stage of prenatal development
    a. conception occurs.
    b. implantation in the uterine wall occurs.
    c. the endoderm, mesoderm, and ectoderm develop.
    d. the mother begins to feel the baby move inside her body.

11. Which of the following have been shown to cause low birth weight?
    a. smoking
    b. alcohol use
    c. cocaine use
    d. all of the above

12. There is good evidence that fathers who _____ harm their baby's prenatal development.
    a. drink alcohol
    b. use aspirin
    c. smoke
    d. all of the above

13. Women should be vaccinated against rubella at least _____ and ideally at least _____ before becoming pregnant.
    a. 1 month; 3 months
    b. 3 months; 6 months
    c. 6 months; 9 months
    d. 9 months; 12 months

Test Solutions

Self-Quiz Solution

1. d (page 47)
2. c (page 47)
3. c (page 50)
4. a (page 54)
5. d (page 56)
6. a (page 58)
7. c (page 62)

8. c (page 64)
9. d (page 69)
10. d (page 72)
11. d (page 76)
12. c (page 77)
13. b (page 78)

Crossword Puzzle Solution

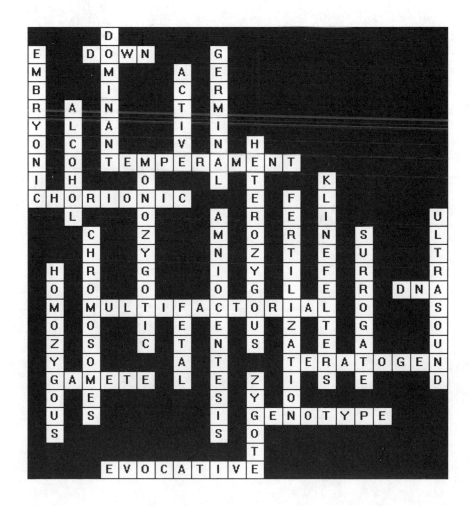

CHAPTER

Birth and the Newborn Infant

INTERESTING AND IMPORTANT THINGS YOU'LL KNOW AFTER READING THIS CHAPTER...

1. How do doctors and nurses quickly determine whether a newborn is healthy? See page 87.

2. What, exactly, do newborns look like? See pages 84 and 87.

3. How safe is it for a woman to take pain-killers during labor? See page 90.

4. How early can a baby be born and still have a chance to survive? See page 98.

5. Why are American babies more likely to die during their first year than babies in other Western countries? See page 104.

6. How well can newborns see and hear? See page 108.

Learning Objectives

When you have mastered the material in this chapter, you should be able to ...

1. Describe the appearance of a neonate. (pages 84 and 87)

2. Understand the progression of labor. (page 85)

3. Specify the five steps of the Apgar test. (page 86)

4. Discuss the phenomenon of bonding. (page 88)

5. Consider the costs and benefits of using anesthesia during delivery. (page 90)

6. Describe 3 alternatives to the traditional, medicalized birth procedure. (page 91)

7. Define the terms low-birthweight baby, small-for-gestational-age baby, and very-low-birth-weight baby. (page 97)

8. Describe the likely short-term and long-term consequences of being born very small or premature. (page 97)

9. Discuss the interventions used to enhance the prognoses for preterm or small infants. (page 99)

10. Delineate the factors that make premature birth more likely. (page 100)

11. Explain the risks of being postmature. (page 101)

12. Describe the advantages and drawbacks to Cesarean delivery. (page 102)

13. Specify the reasons that account for America's high infant mortality rate. (page 104)

14. Describe several of the most important survival reflexes of which newborns are capable. (page 108)

15. Discuss the sensory capabilities of newborn infants. (page 109)

16. Describe neonates' imitative abilities. (page 109)

17. Know how to interact with a newborn. (page 111)

Guided Review

Birth

Labor begins when _____ is released by the mother's pituitary gland. It progresses in _____ stages. The first is the _____ and takes between _____ and _____ hours. Contractions of the greatest intensity occur during _____. By the end of this stage, the _____ has fully opened. During the second stage, the baby moves into the _____ and out of the mother's body. The final part of labor involves expelling the _____ and _____ cord. This takes _____ minutes.

oxytocin (84)
three (85)
longest (85); 16; 24 (85)

transition (85); cervix (85)

birth canal (85)
placenta (86); umbilical (86)
several (86)

Once a baby is born, an _____ test is performed. Scores range from ____ to ____. Babies who score less than ____ need help _____, and those scoring less than ____ need emergency care.

Apgar (86)
0; 10 (87); 7 (87);
breathing (87); 4 (87)

Some people believe that immediate _____ is necessary for good parent-child relationships. There is _____ evidence for this belief.

bonding (88)
little (88)

Most women agree that childbirth is _____. However, drugs can affect the _____ as well as the mother. The American Academy of Pediatrics advocates the _____ of drugs during delivery. They also argue that women should remain in the hospital at least _____ after giving birth.

painful (89)
baby (90)
minimal use (90)

48 hours (91)

Dissatisfaction with traditional practices has led to alternatives. Couples who use the _____ method go through training in which the mother learns to _____ parts of her body. Babies born with the _____ method are immersed in _____ immediately after being born. More and more commonly, couples are choosing to go to _____ rather than hospitals. These centers often employ _____.

Lamaze (91)
relax (91)
Leboyer (92);
warm water (92)
birthing centers (92);
midwives (93)

38 weeks after (97)
7% (97)
5 1/2 pounds (97)
90% (97)
lungs (97)
respiratory (97)

incubators (97); slowly (98)
mild (98)

2 1/4 pounds (98)
30 (98)
24 weeks (98)
expensive (99)

Twins (100)
health (101)
stress (101); Very young (100)

2 weeks (101)
oxygen (101)

Cesarean (102)
fetal distress (102); monitors (102); distress (102)

catecholamines (102)

8.5 (103)
high (103)
twice (104)

increasing (104)
Poverty (104)
prenatal care (104)

Preterm infants are born before _____ conception. About _____ of babies born are this early. These babies weigh less than _____. Small-for-gestational-age babies are born "on time" but weigh _____ or less of what would be expected. Because these babies' _____ have not had time to develop, they can suffer from _____ distress syndrome. To help with this, preterm babies are often placed in _____. These babies develop more_____ than normal and often suffer _____ developmental problems later in life.

Very-low-birth-weight babies weigh less than _____ and have usually been in the womb less than _____ weeks. (The earliest age at which survival is possible is _____.) It is extremely _____ to care for these very small preemies.

Why are some babies born prematurely? _____ often are. The general _____ of the mother also contributes to pre-maturity, as does the mother's _____ level. _____ mothers are especially likely to deliver prematurely.

Postmature babies – those born more than _____ late – are also at risk. In particular, they may not get enough _____.

_____ deliveries, or surgical deliveries, are most often done to relieve _____. Fetal _____ can detect this _____, and so their use is associated with high numbers of Cesareans. Babies born by Cesarean have lower levels of _____ in their blood than babies born vaginally.

The American overall infant mortality rate is about _____ per 1000 births. This is a _____ rate compared to many other countries. African-American babies are _____ as likely as Caucasian babies to die during their first year. This racial difference in infant mortality is _____. _____ is a major contributor to these racial differences. American women in general receive less _____ than women in other countries.

The Competent Neonate

As soon as they are born, infants must begin _____ on their own. In addition, they must begin feeding. Three _____, or unlearned responses, help them do this. The first, _____, allows them to find their mother's nipple. The second, _____, allows them to draw milk into their mouths. The third, _____, lets them get that milk into their stomachs. Some infants, especially those that are _____, develop _____ because they are not yet digesting food properly.

breathing (108)

reflexes (108)
rooting (108)
sucking (108)
swallowing (108)

premature (108); neonatal jaundice (108)

Although their visual _____ is not fully developed, newborn infants can see. They can discriminate different levels of _____ and they have a sense of size _____. They can tell one _____ from another.

acuity (108)

brightness (108); constancy (108); color (109)

Newborns _____ when they hear loud, unexpected noises, and they _____ when they hear other babies cry.

startle (109)
begin crying(109)

Newborns have a _____ sense of touch, and they appear to have a sense of _____ and _____ as well.

fine (109)
taste; smell (109)

Newborns are capable of imitating _____, and they experience different states of _____.

facial expressions (109)
arousal (110)

When first encountering a newborn, do not be surprised at its _____. Hold it _____. Speak _____. And know that its appearance and behavior will change _____ over the next few days.

appearance (111); securely (111); gently (112); greatly (112)

Crossword Puzzle

Birth and the Newborn Infant

Across

4 A white, cheesy substance that covers some babies at birth

6 Small-for-_____ age babies are littler than most babies born at the same age.

8 Babies born more than two weeks before their due date

10 A lack of oxygen

11 The French obstetrician who advocated gentle childbirth

14 Another term for newborn

16 _____-Hicks contractions, or false labor

17 _____, given to a baby immediately after birth

Down

1 Babies born more than two weeks after their due date

2 The infant _____ rate measures the number of infants to die during their first year of life.

3 A dark green, tar-like substance

4 The age of _____ is now about 24 weeks.

5 _____ section: surgically removing the baby from the mother's uterus

7 An incision used to prevent perineal tearing during delivery

9 The fine, downy hair that covers some newborns' bodies

12 The term used to describe the emotional attachment that some believe occurs immediately after a baby's birth

13 Hard-wired, instinctive responses to stimulation

15 The most well-known of the natural childbirth methods

Flash Cards

Describe the appearance of a baby just after birth.

What are Braxton-Hicks contractions and what purpose do they serve

How frequent are labor contractions and how long do they last?

What happens during the first stage of labor?

What is the purpose of an episiotomy?

Which is the easiest stage of labor?

List the five measures of the Apgar scale.

Why is anoxia during delivery so serious a problem?

What is the purpose of vermix?

Why is the concept of bonding harmful?

They are false labor pains, and they serve to ready the uterus for delivery.

They have pointy heads, are covered with blood and vermix, and may have lanugo. Their noses may be squashed.

The cervix opens fully to allow enough room for the baby to pass through.

During the 1st stage of labor, they last between 30 seconds and 2 minutes. They are at first spaced at 8-to-10 minute intervals and then come every 2 minutes.

The third

It widens the vaginal opening.

Because lack of oxygen can cause brain damage.

Appearance (color), pulse (heart rate), grimace (irritability), activity (muscle tone), and respiration (breathing)

Because parents who are separated from their babies might needlessly worry that their relationship with the baby will be damaged.

It is greasy and helps the baby slide through the birth canal.

Describe the birth experience undergone by most American women prior to the 1970s.

Describe how anesthetics can affect the course of labor.

Why is there a trend for women to stay in the hospital for only one day after their baby is born?

What is the purpose of Lamaze training?

What is the main problem faced by babies who are only a little premature?

List 4 problems faced by very premature infants.

What problem can result if premature babies are placed in an incubator with high oxygen levels?

Describe the appearance of a very-low-birthweight baby.

Why is massage beneficial to premature infants?

What two risks are faced by postmature babies?

Contrast breech and transverse positions.

How many American babies are born by Cesarean and how does this compare to other Western countries?

Anesthetics can slow labor down and decrease the baby's oxygen levels.	Women were in a room with other women, and their husbands were not allowed to be with them. They were often given enough medication so that they were unconscious.
The purpose is to teach women to relax when experiencing pain rather than to tense up. This eases labor.	Health insurance companies and managed care providers require women to leave at that time.
(1) Maintaining temperature, (2) breathing, (3) combating infection, (4) a hyper-sensitivity to stimulation	Keeping warm, as they have little fat and cannot regulate their body temperatures.
The eyelids may be fused shut, the ears are only small flaps of skin, and the skin is dark red (regardless of race).	Blindness.
The placenta may not provide enough oxygen and they may become so large that labor is prolonged.	It helps them gain weight, perhaps by providing stimulation and by physiologically arousing them. It may stimulate hormones which cause growth.
About 25% of American babies are born by Cesarean, a rate much higher than in other Western countries.	Breech babies are positioned feet down, whereas transverse babies are lying sideways inside their mothers.

What are two risks to the mother of Cesarean delivery?	How frequent are still births?
List three major reasons why the US infant mortality rate is so high.	How are perspectives on neonatal competency changing?
Name several neonatal reflexes that do not involve feeding.	What visual information do neonates pay the most attention to?
What colors do newborns prefer?	Why can't newborns hear as well as adults?
What use is neonatal ability to imitate facial expression?	How do states of arousal change during infancy?

Less than 1% of babies are stillborn.	Her recovery time is longer, and she is at increased risk of infection.
The trend is to see neonates as more and more competent.	(1) Our high prematurity rate, (2) our high poverty rates, (3) our relative lack of prenatal care for all women
Objects that contrast strongly with their backgrounds.	Neonates can cough, sneeze, and hiccup.
Their ears are not fully developed and the amnionic fluid in their ears must first drain.	Blues and greens
They become more regular and predictable.	It sets the stage for the development of later social interaction.

Practice Test One

1. What is lanugo?
   a. downy hair that covers some newborns' bodies
   b. a waxy, cheesy substance
   c. the opening to the uterus
   d. a dark-green substance passed by the baby during the first few days

2. Transition
   a. occurs at the beginning of the first stage of labor.
   b. occurs at the end of the first stage of labor.
   c. occurs when the baby is actually born.
   d. refers to the first few moments after a baby is born.

3. Which of the following are not measured by the Apgar test?
   a. heart rate
   b. color
   c. irritability
   d. vision

4. The critical period of time in which baby animals are particularly ready to learn from other members of their species is called
   a. bonding.
   b. fenestring.
   c. imprinting.
   d. blazing.

5. About _____ of women indicate that their labors were difficult or very difficult. (They give it a score of 4 or 5 on a 5-point pain scale).
   a. 25%
   b. 50%
   c. 75%
   d. over 90%

6. Which of the following statements is true of Lamaze?
   a. Most parents report their Lamaze births to be a positive experience.
   b. Women are highly medicated during delivery.
   c. The baby is immersed in warm water after it is born.
   d. Lamaze is falling out of favor and becoming less and less common.

7. The average full-term newborn weighs about
   a. 5 1/2 pounds.
   b. 7 1/2 pounds.
   c. 8 1/2 pounds.
   d. 9 1/2 pounds.

8. Approximately _____ of very-low-birthweight babies survive.
   a. 10%
   b. 25%
   c. 50%
   d. 75%

9. Special enhancements to increase the cognitive and social functioning of premature infants should begin
   a. just after birth.
   b. at about 3 months of age.
   c. as soon as they are released from the hospital.
   d. once they begin learning to talk.

10. Which of the following maternal characteristics is *not* associated with premature birth?
    a. very young age
    b. lack of prenatal care
    c. having had previous children
    d. maternal stress

11. Why is postmaturity less of a risk to a baby than prematurity?
    a. Postmaturity can be prevented.
    b. There are no harmful outcomes associated with postmaturity.
    c. Medical treatment after birth can correct most problems associated with postmaturity.
    d. Postmaturity is *not* less of a risk than prematurity.

12. Babies born by Cesarean are somewhat more likely than other babies to
    a. become blind.   c. have trouble breathing.
    b. become deaf.   d. survive.

13. Which change would do the most to decrease American infant mortality?
    a. decrease the incidence of maternal obesity
    b. increase use of birthing centers
    c. institute a national healthcare system
    d. prevent so many postmature births

14. A newborn's brain is _____ of the size it will be as an adult.
    a. 25%   c. 67%
    b. 50%   d. 75%

15. Which of the following statements about newborn's vision is true?
    a. Their vision is blurry.   c. They do not have size constancy.
    b. They cannot see colors.   d. They cannot discriminate brightness.

16. If you stick your tongue out at a newborn, he or she will
    a. cry.   c. stick his or her tongue out at you.
    b. smile.   d. close his or her eyes.

17. Swaddling means to
    a. put your face down close to a baby's face.
    b. speak gently and soothingly.
    c. hold a baby so that his or her head is supported.
    d. wrap a baby tightly in a blanket.

Test Solutions

Self-Quiz Solution

1. a (page 87)
2. b (page 85)
3. d (page 87)
4. c (page 88)
5. c (page 89)
6. a (page 91)
7. b (page 97)
8. c (page 99)
9. a (page 100)
10. c (page 101)
11. a (page 102)
12. c (page 102)
13. c (page 105)
14. a (page 107)
15. a (page 108)
16. c (page 109)
17. d (page 112)

Crossword Puzzle Solution

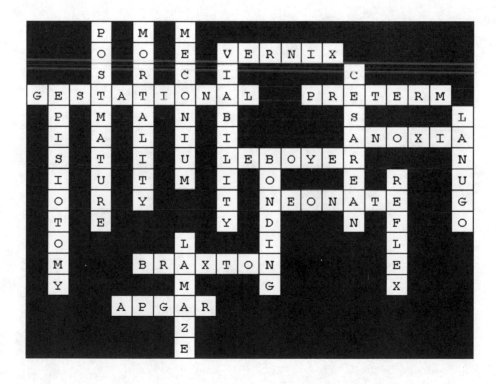

CHAPTER 4

Physical Development in Infancy

INTERESTING AND IMPORTANT THINGS YOU'LL KNOW AFTER READING THIS CHAPTER...

1. Why is it so important that many of baby's brain cells die during infancy? See page 120.

2. Do babies dream when they sleep? See page 124.

3. What fatal disorder kills 7000 US infants each year? See page 125.

4. Why isn't it beneficial for infants to engage in physical exercise? See page 128.

5. How many American children suffer from undernutrition? See page 134.

6. Which is better: bottle or breast feeding? See page 136.

7. How well do infants see? See page 140.

8. Do newborns feel pain? See page 144.

Learning Objectives

When you have mastered the material in this chapter, you should be able to ...

1. Define the four principles of physical growth that dictate an infant's physical development. (page 118)

2. Detail the development of the brain and nervous system. (page 120)

3. Discuss infant sleep patterns and describe how they change with development. (page 123)

4. Describe Sudden Infant Death Syndrome and know which infants are most susceptible to it. (page 125)

5. Understand the uses of, types of, and benefits of reflexes. (page 127)

6. List the ages at which the most important motor milestones are reached. (page 130)

7. Describe the concept of behavioral norms and describe how they vary by ethnicity and culture. (page 131)

8. Detail the scope and importance of infant malnutrition, and to contrast its two major forms. (page 133)

9. Discuss the link between infant and adult obesity. (page 135)

10. Describe the advantages of breast-feeding over bottle-feeding and understand why some women choose to bottle-feed. (page 136)

11. Describe infants' visual abilities and discuss some of the techniques used to study infant visual perception. (page 140)

12. Discuss how well infants hear and know what kinds of auditory discriminations they can make. (page 144)

13. Describe infants' reactions to good and bad tastes and smells. (page 143)

14. Summarize infants' awareness of pain and touch. (page 144)

15. Summarize our knowledge about infants' abilities to integrate information across their senses. (page 145)

16. Know how to appropriately stimulate a baby. (page 146)

Guided Review

Growth and Stability

For the first two years of a person's life, growth is _____. In fact, babies double their birth weight by _____ and triple it, to _____ pounds, by _____. By two years of age, most infants are about _____ tall.

rapid (118)
5 months
22 (118); 1 year (118)
3 feet (118)

The _____ principle of development states that a baby's _____ will grow before its legs. The _____ principle indicates that body parts near the baby's _____ will grow prior to its _____. The principle of _____ integration holds that simple skills develop _____ at first but then merge and become more _____. Lastly, the principle of _____ of systems describes the fact that different organ systems grow at _____ rates.

cephalocaudal (118)
head (118); proximodistal (119)
trunk
extremities (119); hierarchical (119); independently (119); complex (119)
independence (120)
different (120)

Infants are born with between _____ nerve cells, or _____. _____ new neurons are created after birth. After birth, many of these neurons _____ so that the others have room to grow larger. Another way that nerve cells change is that they develop a _____ coat. The brain is highly _____, and the _____ in good part shapes its final configuration.

100 and 200 billion (120)
neurons (120); No (120)
die (120)

myelin (120)
plastic (121); environment (121)

Some _____ — repetitive, _____ patterns of behavior – are present at birth and others develop over the _____. One such behavior is sleeping. On average, newborns sleep _____ per day, usually divided into _____ stretches. Babies spend more time _____ than do adults and older children. It probably functions as _____. Infant sleep patterns are affected by _____ practices.

rhythms (122); cyclical (122)

1st year (122)
16-17 hours (123)
2-hour (124) REMing (124)
autostimulation (125)
cultural (125)

SIDS is a disorder in which infants die in their _____ because they stop _____.

sleep (125)
breathing (126)

Motor Development

reflexes (127)
survival (127); swimming (127)
eye-blink (127)

voluntary (128); more quickly
(128)
advanced (129); caregiving
(129)

gross motor (130)
backwards (130); 6 to 8 (130)

supported (130); unassisted
(130); 6 months; (130) fine
motor (130)
4 months (130)

Brazelton Neonatal (131)

culture (131)
later (131)
close (131)
early (131)

similar (131)

Newborns come into the world able to perform unlearned _____. Some of these clearly have or at one time had _____ value. For example, the _____ reflex causes babies in water to paddle and kick; the _____ reflex protects the eye. Reflexes disappear as behavior becomes more _____. Babies who practice reflexes develop _____ than other babies, but ultimately are no more motorily _____. Reflexes can help promote _____ by the parents.

Movements that involve large areas of the body are called _____ movements. By six months, many infants can move _____, while by _____ months they can crawl. By 9 or 10 months, most infants can walk if they are _____; by one year, they can walk _____. Sitting without support emerges at about _____. In contrast, _____ skills involve more precise movements. For example, babies begin to precisely reach at about _____. A test used to determine whether infants are developing normatively is the _____ Behavioral Assessment Scale.

The pace of motor development is influenced by _____. For example, Ache children walk _____ than others because they are kept _____ to their mothers. Conversely, Kipsigis children walk _____ because their mothers give them practice and encouragement. In the long run, the infants' motor skills become _____.

Nutrition in Infancy: Fueling Motor Development

cognitive; social (133);
long-lasting (134)

marasmus (134)
kwashiorkor (134)
One quarter (133)
undernutrition (134)
cognitive (134); Failure to (134)

no more (135)

fat cells (136)

Infants suffering from malnutrition suffer from physical, _____, and _____ delays. The effects may be _____ even if diet is improved.

Two types of malnutrition are _____, in which the body wastes away, and _____, which is marked by bloating and swelling. _____ of American families with young children live in poverty and are at risk for _____. This can have long-term effects on _____ development. _____ thrive is a medical condition leading to malnutrition.

Infants who are obese are _____ likely to be obese as adults than other infants. These babies may lay down additional _____, however.

_____ is the preferred food for young infants. It offers all necessary _____ and confers _____ to some illnesses. It is more easily _____. Breast-feeding is also beneficial to the _____, as it is associated with lowered _____ rates. About _____ of mothers do not breast-feed, however, due to factors such as _____ status and _____.

Breast milk (136)
nutrients (136); immunity (136)
digested (136)
mother; cancer (136);
1/2 (137)
socioeconomic (137); health (137)

Most infants should begin solid foods between _____ months.

4 to 6

The Development of the Senses

Estimates of newborns' visual acuity ranges from _____ to _____. By _____ months of age, it has become 20/20. Binocular vision develops by about _____. Studies using the _____ have allowed researchers to study babies' depth perception. As early as _____, infants will refuse to crawl to the cliff's deep side. By _____, infants show preferences for particular types of visual stimuli and can even recognize _____.

20/200,
20/600 (140); 6 (141)
14 weeks (141)
visual cliff (141)
6 months (141)

just after birth (141)
their mother's faces (142)

Infants can hear _____. They are _____ sensitive to high and low frequencies than adults. They are _____ sensitive to middle-range frequencies. Infants can localize sounds as well as adults by the time they are _____. _____ month-olds can tell if a melody changes by even a single note. Infants as young as _____ will dishabituate when words are changed by just one sound, and by _____ months, they can discriminate between passages read in Spanish or in English. _____ recognize the sound of their mothers' voices.

before birth (141); more (141)
less (141)

1 year (141)
6- (141)
1 to 4 months (141)
5 (141)

Newborns (141)

Babies less than 2 weeks old can recognize their mothers by _____ alone, but only if they had been _____. Even young infants dislike _____ tastes and like _____ ones.

odor (144); breast-fed (144);
bitter (144); sweet (144)

_____ produces signs of distress in newborns; for example, they begin to _____ and their heart rate _____. Often, however, there is a _____ in the response.

Pain (144)
sweat (144); increases (144);
delay (144)

Gentle _____ can soothe a crying infant. Many of the basic _____ newborns perform are triggered by it.

touch (145)
reflexes (145)

multimodal (145)

one- (145)

positions (146); explore (146)
rough and tumble (146); touch
(146); toys (146)

The _____ approach to perception considers how information collected by the different sense is integrated and coordinated. Even _____ month-olds demonstrate some ability to do this.

Good advice for parents who wish to ensure that their children develop good motor abilities includes: carry your baby in different _____; let him or her _____; engage him or her in _____ play; let your baby _____ his food; and provide stimulating _____.

Crossword Puzzle

Physical Development in Infancy

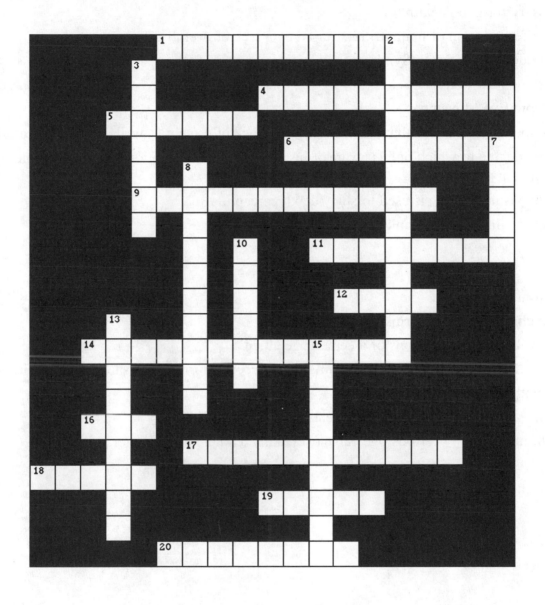

Across

5   The principle of _____ organization

22 The ability to integrate and make sense of sensory information

24 A fatty substance that covers nerve cells

30 An awareness of one's environment

36 A condition in which a person does not ingest enough of the food stuffs, vitamins, etc., necessary for good health

45 A specific form of malnutrition caused by a lack of overall calories

51 Sudden Infant Death Syndrome

58 From "near to far"

67 Rapid Eye Movement

72 A specific form of malnutrition caused by a lack of protein as well as a lack of calories

73 The degree to which one is aware of his or her internal condition and the surrounding environment

78 The visual _____ is used to study depth perception.

84 Inborn, instinctive simple behaviors

Down

14 From "head to tail"

19 Cyclical, repetitive forms of behavior

31 Levels that most persons of a certain age attain

33 The ability to grow and respond differently according to the pressures of the environment

44 Another name for nerve cell

55 The _____ Neonatal Assessment Inventory

59 During _____ periods one can most readily learn a new behavior.

Flash Cards

Does physical growth occur continuously or does it occur in spurts?	List the four principles of physical growth.
In addition to size, what do the principles of cephalocaudal and proximodistal development refer to?	Give an example of the principle of hierarchical organization.
How do neurons change after birth?	What determines which neurons grow and which die during development?
Give several examples of infant states.	Name two ways that REM sleep changes with development.
List some of the risk factors for SIDS.	Describe the Babinski reflex.

The principle of cephalocaudal development; the principle of proximodistal development; the principle of hierarchical organization; the principle of independence	It occurs in spurts, separated by periods of several days.
One must first be able to reach and to grab, separately, before one can reach and pick up a toy.	To the development of strength, coordination, myelinization, and control
The amount of stimulation they receive	Although they do not become more numerous, they increase in size, become covered with myelin, and become arranged by function.
Babies do relatively less and less of it and it becomes associated with dreaming.	Crying, fussing, being alert, sleeping
It occurs when you touch the side of a baby's foot; it will splay it's toes out.	Boys, African-American babies, low-birthweight babies, babies with low Apgar scores, and babies whose mothers smoked during pregnancy

How do we know that performing reflexes exercises the body and prepares it for more advanced behavior?

Why might it be harmful to encourage a baby to engage in structured exercise?

Describe a reflex useful for other primates but not particularly so for human infants.

What is the social import of many infant reflexes?

Trace the development of locomotory skills.

What is the major limitation of the Brazelton Neonatal Behavior Assessment Scale?

Does the fact that there is cultural variation in the rate at which infants motorily develop prove that these differences are environmental?

Why was bottle-feeding preferred in the 1940s?

Describe how breast-feeding helps mothers.

Why is breast-feeding particularly preferable in Third World nations?

What is the best way to add solids to an infant's diet?

Contrast the terms sensation and perception.

Because overuse of muscles can cause muscle strain, fractured bones, and dislocated limbs	Because comparisons between babies who practice performing reflexes and those who do not show that the babies who do practice master similar, voluntary movements earlier.
Parents find it very rewarding to have their infants respond to them, even if that response is reflexive. Therefore, reflexes can help with parent-child attachment.	The Moro reflex involves the infant grabbing onto something above it when it feels it is falling. This is useful for baby monkeys who cling to their mothers' fur.
That it is normed on a white, middle-class sample	At first infants move backwards. By 6 months they can move forward and by 8-10 months crawl. They walk with support at 9-11 months and alone by a year.
Because doctors thought that it was important for mothers to keep track of how much milk their babies consumed	No, because persons in these different cultures vary genetically as well as environmentally
Women in these countries often have only polluted water to mix in with the formula.	Women who breast-feed have: lower cancer rates; more quickly-shrinking uteruses; inhibited ovulation; lower stress hormone levels; enjoyable experiences with it.
Sensation is the stimulation of the sense organs; perception is the analysis and interpretation of sensations.	One should only gradually introduce solids, beginning with cereals, and then fruits and then vegetable products.

Describe babies' responses to the visual cliff.

Why do children lose the ability to so clearly hear very high and very low frequency sounds?

Why are young infants at a disadvantage, relative to adults, in localizing sound?

How can an infant's tendency to habituate be used to study his perceptual abilities?

How do we know that infants like sweet tastes?

Name two smells that infants like.

Why do infants like to place things in their mouths?

How do we know that one-month old infants can integrate sight and touch?

Probably due to loud noise exposure.	Two- and three-month olds' heart beats speed up; infants 6 months and older refuse to crawl over the edge to the deep side.
Infants habituate (become bored) with repeated stimulation; however, if they can perceive a change in the stimulus, they will regain interest.	Their ears are closer together since their heads are smaller; therefore there is less of a difference in the time that sound reaches their two ears.
Bananas and butter	Because they smile when eating something sweet and suck harder to drink sweet-tasting liquids
Because they will look longer at something they have sucked on than something they have not	Their mouths are very sensitive to touch.

Practice Test One

1. According to the proximodistal principle, which of the following abilities develops last?
   a. the ability to move one's fingers
   b. the ability to lift one's head
   c. the ability to bend at the waist
   d. the ability to bend one's knees

2. Martina was born completely blind due to severe cataracts in her eyes. The cataracts were surgically removed when she was three. What is the likely outcome of this surgery?
   a. Martina will be able to see perfectly normally.
   b. Martina will be able to see only in strongly light.
   c. Martina will never be able to see colors.
   d. Martina will probably not be able to see even if her eyes are now functioning normally.

3. Most babies sleep through the night by
   a. one month of age.
   b. 5 months of age.
   c. 1 year of age.
   d. 2 years of age.

4. Who is SIDS most likely to strike?
   a. healthy 1-year olds
   b. healthy babies during the first 6 months of life
   c. ill, frail babies during the first 3 months of life
   d. any child through age 2

5. Which reflex consists of a baby's throwing out her arms and trying to grasp something when she feels she is falling?
   a. the tonic neck reflex
   b. the swimming reflex
   c. the Moro reflex
   d. the Babinski reflex

6. Babies begin to walk with support when they are about:
   a. 6 months old
   b. 8 months old
   c. 10 months old
   d. 12 months old

7. African American infants show _____ motor development than Caucasian infants.
   a. slower
   b. more rapid
   c. more variable
   d. less predictable

8. Marasmus is most likely to strike
   a. healthy, active infants.
   b. young infants.
   c. older children.
   d. obese children.

9. Obese infants
   a. probably drink breast milk.
   b. are very much more likely to be obese as adults.
   c. have more fat cells for the rest of their lives.
   d. all of the above.

10. High levels of DHA in the brain are associated with babies
    a. who are early crawlers and walkers.
    b. who are premature.
    c. who have kwashiorkor.
    d. who have been breast-fed.

11. Depth perception relies upon
    a. binocular vision.
    b. sharp visual acuity.
    c. multimodal sensory abilities.
    d. habituation.

12. Newborn infants can recognize
    a. their mother's voice.
    b. their father's voice.
    c. both their mother's and their father's voices.
    d. neither voice until they are three months of age.

13. Babies begin to positively respond to sweet tastes
    a. when they are very young.
    b. at three months.
    c. at five months.
    d. when they begin to eat solid food.

14. How has our understanding of infants' reactions to pain changed?
    a. We now believe that infants do not experience intense pain.
    b. We now believe that infants experience only a few painful stimuli.
    c. We now believe that infants can and do experience some pain.
    d. We now believe that infants experience pain even more intensely than adults.

15. We know that newborns can
    a. recognize by sight things they have heard.
    b. recognize by touch things they have seen.
    c. recognize by sight things they have touched.
    d. all of the above

16. Infants who walk early
    a. are no more advanced at two years than infants who do not.
    b. are cognitively advanced at two years and continue to be throughout childhood.
    c. are cognitively advanced at two but then other children catch up.
    d. are socially advanced at two.

Test Solutions

Self-Quiz Solution

1.	a	(page 119)	
2.	d	(page 121)	
3.	c	(page 124)	
4.	b	(page 126)	
5.	c	(page 129)	
6.	c	(page 130)	
7.	b	(page 131)	
8.	b	(page 134)	

9. c (page 136)

10. d (page 137)

11. a (page 141)

12. a (page 143)

13. a (page 144)

14. c (page 144)

15. c (page 145)

16. a (page 146)

Crossword Puzzle Solution

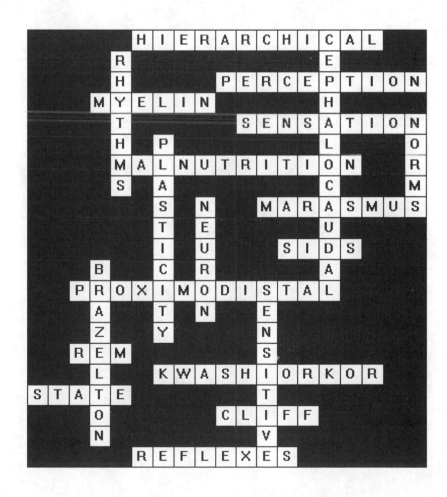

CHAPTER 5

Cognitive Development in Infancy

INTERESTING AND IMPORTANT THINGS YOU'LL KNOW AFTER READING THIS CHAPTER...

1. How and why do people develop strong feelings about objects and events? See page 161.

2. How early can infants learn? See page 163.

3. Can any adult remember his or her infancy? How old are our oldest memories? See page 165.

4. What makes an infant smart? Are some smarter than others? See page 166.

5. What can you do to help ensure that an infant will become intelligent? See page 169.

6. What good is "baby talk"? See page 178.

Learning Objectives

When you have mastered the material in this chapter, you should be able to ...

1. Give an overview of the major principles of Piaget's theory of cognitive development. (page 152)

2. Detail the developmental changes in each of the six stages of the sensorimotor period of development. (page 153)

3. Discuss the strengths and weaknesses of Piaget's beliefs. (page 157)

4. Understand the role of learning — classical conditioning, operant conditioning, and habituation — in human development. (page 161)

5. Describe the three limitations on infants' ability to learn. (page 163)

6. Discuss the ways and reasons that memory improves over the course of infancy. (page 164)

7. Discuss the controversy surrounding infantile amnesia. (page 165)

8. Give an overview of the different approaches to infant intelligence. (page 166)

9. Describe the roles of visual-recognition memory and cross-modal transference in infant intelligence. (page 168)

10. Outline steps that can be taken to help promote infant cognitive development. (page 169)

11. Explain prelinguistic communication — the communication means babies use before they can speak. (page 172)

12. Describe the earliest linguistic utterances: holophrases and telegraphic speech. (page 174)

13. Contrast the two major approaches to language acquisition: the learning theory approach and Chomsky's language acquisition device. (page 177)

14. List the features of motherese, and to understand how and why it is used. (page 178)

15. Assess an infant's language development. (page 181)

Guided Review

Piaget's Approach to Cognitive Development

Piaget believed that knowledge is the product of direct _____ behavior: infants learn by _____. Piaget believed that children pass through _____ stages of cognitive development as they mature, the first of which is the _____ period. In his view, _____ are organized patterns of sensorimotor functioning. Cognitive growth occurs because children _____ some new information by applying old schemes; in addition, they _____ to other new information by changing their ways of thinking.

motor; doing (152)
four (152)

sensorimotor (152); schemes (152)
assimilate (153)
accommodate (153)

The sensorimotor period is divided into _____ substages. The first consists of simple _____. During the second substage, which lasts from _____ months, infants acquire habits and _____ circular reactions. During the 3rd substage, which lasts from _____ months, infants develop _____ circular reactions. These differ from the primary circular reactions in that they are focused _____. During the 4th substage, which lasts from _____ months, infants learn to _____ their schemes and begin to employ _____ behavior. A rudimentary understanding of _____ also develops at this time. During the 5th substage, which lasts from _____ months, infants perform _____ circular reactions in which they _____ what they do with objects. Finally, during the final sensorimotor substage, which lasts from _____ months, infants develop mental _____ of their worlds and begin to perform _____ imitation.

six (153)
reflexes (153)
1 to 4 (154)
primary (154)
4 to 8 (154)
secondary (154)
outwards (154)

8 to 12 (155)
coordinate (155)
goal-directed (155)
object permanence (156);
12 to 18 (156)
tertiary (156); vary (157)

18 to 24 (158)
representations (158);
deferred (158)

How accurate was Piaget? Children do learn about the world by _____ on objects. His basic _____ is also probably correct. On the other hand, many researchers now feel that development is more _____ than Piaget thought, and less grounded in _____ activities alone. When researchers use more sophisticated techniques or go to different cultures, they find that infants often perform tasks at a _____ than Piaget believed.

acting (157); sequence (158)

continuous (158)
motor (158)

younger age (159)

store (161)
quantitative (161)

Information processors are interested in the ways that we take in, use, and _____ information. They tend to focus on _____ changes in ability.

neutral (161); Ivan Pavlov (161); substitution (162)
paired (162)
birth (162)

In classical condition, an organism learns to respond to a _____ stimulus. It was discovered by _____. Classical conditioning depends upon stimulus _____, which occurs when two stimuli are _____. Infants can be classically conditioned at _____.

Operant (162)
consequence (162)
birth (162)

_____ conditioning occurs when a response is strengthened or weakened depending upon its _____. It is present from _____.

habituation (163)
decreases (163)

birth (163)

The most primitive form of learning is _____. This occurs when a response _____ after repeated presentation of a stimulus without consequence. It is present from _____.

memory (164)
longer (164); hints (164)

hippocampus (165)

Without _____, infants could not learn. It improves during the course of infancy in that it lasts _____ and _____ become more effective. The part of the brain most involved in infant memories is the _____.

third (165)

Most people cannot remember events prior to their _____ birthday. Although the physical traces of memory are likely _____, it is hard to retrieve them due to _____.

permanent (165); interference (165)
disagree (166)

Psychologists _____ as to what constitutes infant intelligence. The earliest infant developmental norms were devised by _____. He developed the developmental _____. More commonly used are the _____ Scales of Infant Development, which focus on both _____ and _____ abilities. These scales do a _____ job at predicting adult functioning.

Gesell (166)
quotient (166); Bayley (167)
mental;
motor (167); poor (167)

speed (168)
habituation (168); visual-recognition (168)
cross-modal (168)

The infant ability that correlates best with later adult intelligence is processing _____. Therefore, infants' scores on _____ and _____ memory tests correlate with later intelligence. Similar, infants who display high levels of _____ transference tend to develop into bright children.

In order to promote cognitive growth, parents should let infants _____ their world and should be _____ to them. Parents should _____ to their infants, and should not _____ them too hard.

explore (169); responsive (169); read (170)
push (170)

The Roots of Language

Language, a meaningful arrangement of _____, is the primary way humans communicate. In general, language _____ precedes language _____.

symbols (172)

comprehension (172); production (172)

Prelinguistic communication relies upon _____, sounds, and _____. Babbling begins at about _____ months and continues until a child is about _____. At about 5 months, _____ are added to the babbled sounds; by 6 months, you can tell what language a child is _____.

gestures (173)
facial expressions (173); 2 (174); 1 year (174)
consonants (174)
speaking (174)

First words are usually spoken between _____ months. By 15 months, most children have a _____ word vocabulary. This _____ stage usually ends at about _____, usually just about the time there is an increase in vocabulary to about _____ words.

10 and 14 (174)
10- (175)
holophrastic (175); 18 months (175)
400 (175)

Children's first sentences are called _____ speech. At this time, children frequently _____ words – that is, use them too narrowly, and they also _____ words, or use them too generally.

telegraphic (176)
underextend (176)
overextend (176)

There are two very _____ approaches to language acquisition. The _____ theory approach says that children learn language because they are rewarded for speaking. This theory has trouble explaining how children learn language's _____. The second theory, pioneered by Noam _____, says that language is _____. He proposed a neural system called the _____ device which allows for easy language acquisition, and believes that all languages share a _____.

different (177)
learning (177)

rules (177)
Chomsky (177); innate (177)
language- acquisition (177)

universal grammar (177)

Most people use _____ when speaking to infants. It is high _____, intonation is _____, words are _____, and its sentences are short and _____. Newborns _____ such speech.

motherese (178)
pitched (178); varied (178); concrete (178); simple (178); prefer (178)

diminutives (179)
firmly (179)

6 months (181)
6 (181)
gestures (181)
pretend (181)

Parents speak to their sons and daughters differently. For example, girls hear more _____ than boys. Also, boys are spoken to more _____ and directly.

Children develop language at different rates. However, children should be able to discriminate some speech from other speech by _____. Also, children should continue to produce their own sounds after _____ months of age. They should use _____ to communicate, and they should babble and _____ to speak.

Crossword Puzzle

Cognitive Development in Infancy

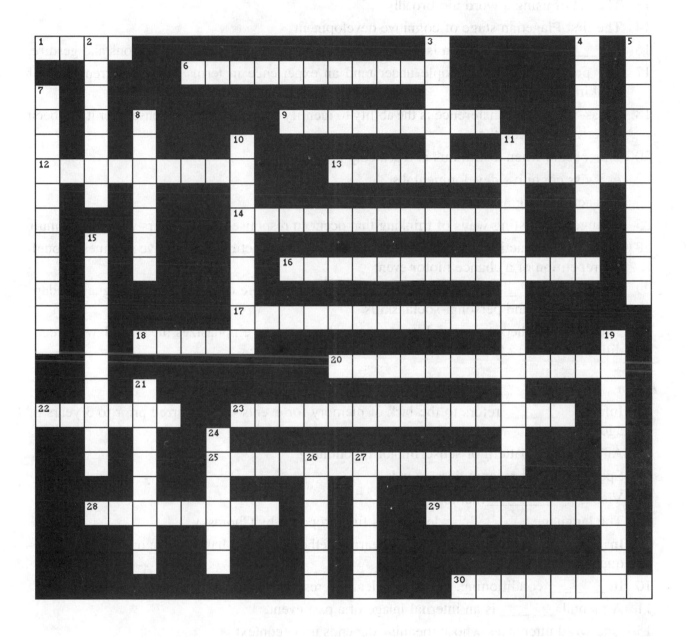

Across

1   _____-directed behaviors are behaviors in which several schemes are combined and coordinated.

6   _____ speech leaves out all noncritical words.

9   The type of speech that adults use when speaking to infants

12   _____ grammar: the simple underlying structure shared by all the world's languages.

13   The act of using a word too broadly

14   The first Piagetian stage of cognitive development

16   _____ communication is accomplished through sounds, facial expressions and gesture.

17   The process by which people understand an experience in terms of their current way of thinking

18   Cross-_____ transference is the ability to identify something in one sense after it has been experienced in another.

20   This occurs when a stimulus is repeatedly presented.

22   A Swiss cognitive developmentalist

23   The act of using a word too restrictively

25   Changes in existing ways of thinking that occur in response to encounters with new stimuli

28   _____ reaction: an activity that permits the construction of cognitive schemes through the repetition of a chance motor event

29   Developmental _____: an overall developmental score of motor skills, language, adaptive behavior, and personal-social skills

30   The _____ theory approach to language development emphasizes the basic laws of conditioning.

Down

2   Infantile _____ refers to the lack of memory for events that occurred prior to 3 years of age.

3   An organized pattern of sensorimotor functioning

4   Speech-like but meaningless sounds

5   Visual - _____memory

7   The language _____ device was first proposed by Chomsky.

8   In _____ conditioning, individuals learn whether an action has positive or negative consequences.

10   In _____ conditioning, individuals learn to respond to previously neutral stimuli.

11   A mental _____ is an internal image of a past event.

15   One word utterances whose meaning depends upon context

19   The _____-processing approach to cognition seeks to understand the ways that individuals take in, use, and store information.

21   _____ imitation is imitation that occurs some time after an infant witnesses an event.

24   The _____ Scales of Infant Development

26   The process by which information is recorded, stored, and retrieved

27   _____ permanence is mastered when an infant will search for a completely hidden object

Flash Cards

List Piaget's four stages of cognitive development.	According to Piaget, what is needed for cognitive development to occur?
Why do children perform circular reactions?	Contrast primary and secondary circular reactions.
Discuss Robert Siegler's view of cognitive development.	How did Karen Wynn demonstrate that even 5-month-olds have a rudimentary conception of addition?
What explanations in addition to a lack of object permanence can be used to explain why young infants don't search for hidden objects?	Contrast the Piagetian and information-processing approaches to cognitive development.
Who was Little Albert?	How do researchers measure habituation?

Physical maturation and appropriate environmental experiences	The sensorimotor period, the preoperational period, the concrete operational period, and the formal operational period
Primaries are centered on the child's own body, whereas secondaries are focused on the effects the child can produce in the world.	Because they are pleasurable
By showing that they would look longer when only one toy was present even though two had been placed behind the screen	Siegler believes that development occurs in waves, rather than abruptly or continuously.
Piaget looked at qualitative, major milestones of development; information-producers seek more fine-grained, quantitative change.	They may lack the memory to know where the object was hidden or they may lack motor control to get it.
By looking at changes in sucking rates, gaze duration, heart rate and breathing rate	Little Albert was a boy who was classically conditioned to fear white, furry objects by John Watson.

What are the three limits on infant learning?

How do we know that even newborns have some memory?

What four measures make up Gesell's developmental quotient?

Of what use are developmental scales? What are they not good at?

Give an example of classical conditioning in infancy.

Give an example of operant conditioning in infancy.

In what order are sounds added to babbling?

How is meaning determined when a child is using holophrases?

Describe the content of most telegraphic sentences.

What kinds of words are left out of telegraphic speech?

What are two problems with the learning theory approach to language acquisition?

What evidence is there that language is not a uniquely human phenomenon?

Because they can learn, something that would be impossible if they couldn't remember previous experiences	(1) The infants' behavioral state, (2) natural constraints (physical and perceptual limitations), (3) motivational constraints
Developmental scales are useful to screen for infants who need intervention; they do not predict adult intelligence.	Motor skills, language use, adaptive behavior, and personal-social behavior
An infant learns that her father will continue playing with her if she gurgles at him.	An infant learns to cry as soon as he hears the bathtub water running (assuming that he hates baths).
By the context the word is spoken in.	First are vowel sounds, then lip consonants (e.g., b and p) are added, then tongue consonants (e.g., d and n) and finally nasal and dental sounds (e.g., m and f)
Grammatical words, such as auxiliary verbs, prepositions, articles, conjunctions, etc.	They are comments and observations, not requests or questions.
Research has shown that apes can learn simple, basic language forms.	First, children are reinforced for ungrammatical as well as grammatical utterances; second, it can't explain how children learn language's rules.

Why is "motherese" an inappropriate term?	Why might adults use motherese when speaking to infants?

Because infants prefer it and
because it might help infants learn
language better than regular speech

Because fathers and non-parents
use it as well as mothers

Practice Test One

1. Erika enjoys eating cookies because they taste good. At lunch yesterday, her mother gave her an oatmeal cookie to eat – a particular kind she had never had before. Still, Erika ate it and thought it tasted great. This is an example of
   a. assimilation.
   b. habituation.
   c. motherese.
   d. accommodation.

2. Lee has recently begun to perform intentional, goal-directed actions such as opening a box to get to the toy inside it. Lee is probably about
   a. 3 months old.
   b. 6 months old.
   c. 9 months old.
   d. 1 year old.

3. Which of the following is the most serious criticism leveled against Piaget's theory?
   a. That children do not assimilate information.
   b. That children do not grow in abrupt spurts.
   c. That children cannot usually accomplish his tasks until older than he claimed.
   d. That his sequence was incorrect.

4. Quentin used to wake up whenever the hall phone rang, but now he sleeps through the ringing. This is probably because
   a. he has become a deeper sleeper.
   b. he has habituated to the sound.
   c. he has been operantly conditioned to ignore the sound.
   d. he has no memory of the phone previously ringing.

5. In order to learn, a baby must
   a. be awake and alert.
   b. be able to perceive the stimulus.
   c. be motivated to respond.
   d. all of the above

6. Phil is a 3-month-old baby. Which of the following is likely true?
   a. Phil has virtually no memory.
   b. Phil cannot use hints and retrieval cues to help him remember.
   c. Phil forgets information more quickly than his older sister.
   d. All of the above are true.

7. Which is the best evidence that memories laid down in infancy are permanent?
   a. Most adults can remember events that occurred when they were young infants.
   b. Preschoolers can remember events that occurred when they were infants.
   c. Interference does not become significant until adulthood.
   d. The hippocampus is mature at birth.

8. The earliest researcher to develop normative infant developmental scales was
   a. Nancy Bayley.
   b. Robert Siegler.
   c. Arnold Gesell.
   d. Jean Piaget.

9. The infant cognitive ability that best predicts later intelligence is
   a. language use.
   b. long-term memory capacity.
   c. short-term memory capacity.
   d. processing speed.

10. Piaget and information-processors would both agree that
    a. infants learn by actively doing.
    b. cognitive development is qualitative.
    c. cognitive development occurs gradually and continuously.
    d. memory improvement is the key to cognitive development.

11. Prelinguistic babies show evidence of
    a. grammar.
    b. turn-taking.
    c. production.
    d. extending.

12. Children begin producing sentences at about
    a. 12 months.
    b. 15 months.
    c. 18 months.
    d. 24 months.

13. Which of the following are not major part of Chomsky's theory of language acquisition?
    a. reward
    b. universal grammar
    c. language-acquisition device
    d. innate mechanisms

14. Which of the following is not a feature of motherese?
    a. It is repetitive.
    b. It is spoken rapidly.
    c. It is spoken with a sing-song intonation.
    d. It is spoken with a high-pitched voice.

15. Carl began babbling when he was 3 months old, but now that he is 7 months old he has stopped. What is your reaction?
    a. Carl is developing perfectly normally.
    b. You are not worried; his behavior is a little unusual, but as long as he once babbled he's probably fine.
    c. You are pleased because you believe that Carl is developing more rapidly than normal.
    d. You are worried because you fear Carl may be deaf.

Test Solutions

Self-Quiz Solution

1. a (page 153)
2. c (page 155)
3. b (page 158)
4. b (page 163)
5. d (page 163)
6. c (page 164)
7. b (page 165)
8. c (page 166)

9. d (page 168)
10. a (page 169)
11. b (page 173)
12. c (page 175)
13. a (page 177)
14. b (page 178)
15. d (page 181)

Crossword Puzzle Solution

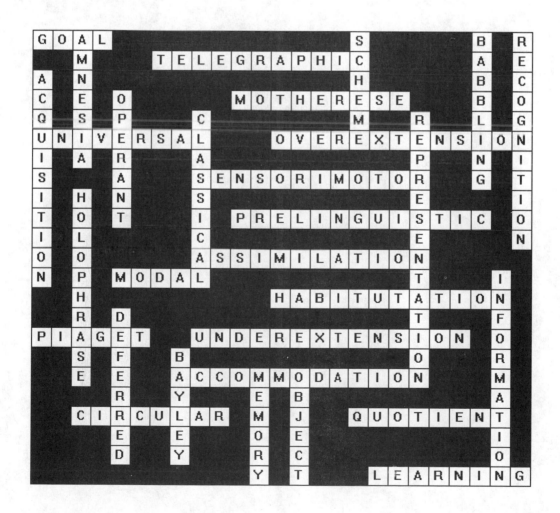

CHAPTER 6

Social and Personality Development in Infancy

INTERESTING AND IMPORTANT THINGS YOU'LL KNOW AFTER READING THIS CHAPTER...

1. Do infants experience emotions? See page 190.

2. Can infants tell how you're feeling? See page 193.

3. Do infants have friends? See page 204.

4. Why do boys and girls — even as infants — behave differently? See page 209.

5. How can you know whether a day-care center is of high quality? See page 212.

FORMING THE ROOTS OF SOCIABILITY

Emotions in infancy: Do infants experience emotional highs and lows?

Social referencing: Feeling what others feel

The development of self: Do infants know who they are?

Theory of mind: Infants' perspectives on the mental lives of others — and themselves

FORGING RELATIONSHIPS

Attachment: Forming social bonds

Are there cross-cultural differences in attachment?

Producing attachment: The roles of mother, father, and infant

Infant interactions: Developing a working relationship

Infants' sociability with their peers: Infant-infant interaction

Infants teaching infants: When babies become experts

DIFFERENCES AMONG INFANTS

Personality development: The characteristics that make infants unique

Temperament: Stabilities in infant behavior

Gender: Why do boys wear blue and girls wear pink?

Family life in the 1990s: Ozzie and Harriet go the way of the dinosaurs

Infant day care: Assessing the consequences

Choosing the right infant care provider

Learning Objectives

When you have mastered the material in this chapter, you should be able to ...

1. Answer the question of whether infants experience and display emotions. (page 190)

2. Contrast stranger and separation anxiety. (page 191)

3. Discuss how smiling changes during the first two years of life. (page 192)

4. Describe infants' abilities to detect other people's emotions. (page 193)

5. Explain what is meant by "social referencing." (page 193)

6. Describe the roots of self-awareness. (page 194)

7. Describe the nature of infants' theory of mind. (page 195)

8. Discuss the causes of infant attachment. (page 197)

9. Contrast the four different forms of attachment. (page 198)

10. Understand the cause and meaning of cultural attachment differences. (page 199)

11. Contrast the contributions of mother's behavior, father's behavior, and infant's behavior in determining the nature of attachment. (page 200)

12. Discuss the concept of reciprocal socialization. (page 203)

13. Describe infants' interactions with each other. (page 204)

14. Summarize Erikson's theory of personality development during infancy. (page 207)

15. Explain what is meant by "temperament" and describe the three main types of temperaments. (page 208)

16. Describe the emergence of gender differences during infancy. (page 209)

17. Enumerate the ways in which the American family has changed since the 1950s. (page 211)

18. Discuss the pros and cons of placing infants into day care. (page 212)

19. List the qualities that distinguish high-quality from low-quality day care. (page 214).

Guided Review

Forming the Roots of Sociability

Infants can produce a variety of facial _____ and these displays are _____ across cultures. Although it is not certain, most researchers believe that infants _____ experience emotions. _____ emotions theory proposes that expressions help regulate emotional experiences.

expressions (190)
similar (190)
do (191)
Differential (191)

At the age of 6 or 7 months, most infants develop some degree of _____ anxiety and begin to dislike unfamiliar persons. Similarly, most develop some degree of _____ anxiety and are distressed when their caretaker leaves them.

stranger (191)
separation (192)

Infants' first smiles are _____. By two months, however, they develop _____ smiles. As they get older, their smiling becomes more and more _____.

reflexive (192)
social (192)
selective (192)

Infants can discriminate sad from happy voices by the time they are _____ months old; this is slightly _____ than they can decode facial expressions.

5 (193); earlier (193)

Children engage in social _____ when they are uncertain as to how to react. It begins at about _____ months. They do this by attending to others' _____.

referencing (193)
8 or 9 (193)
facial expressions (194)

Infants begin to recognize themselves in a mirror at about _____ months of age. At about this same time they begin to have some understanding of their own _____.

17-24 (194)
capabilities (194)

One's knowledge and beliefs about the mental world constitute one's _____. The rudiments of _____ — the tendency to feel what another is feeling — develops very early at _____ months.

theory of mind (195); empathy (195)
2 (195)

Attachment (197)

imprinting (197)
innate (197)

oral (197); Bowlby's (197)
cuddly (197)

security (197)

Ainsworth (197)
four (198)
securely (198)
Avoidant (198); are wary of
(198); ambivalent (198); positive; negative (198)
disoriented (199)
lifelong (199)

cultural (199)

independence (200)

responsive (20)
temperament (201)
expressivity (201); mixed (201)

different (202)
playing (202); caring (202)
roughly (203)

jointly (203)
mutually (203)

interested (204)
more (204)
games (204); imitate (204)
teach (205)

_____ is the most important social bond formed during infancy. This human behavior is in some ways similar to animal _____ and suggests that the tendency to form these bonds might be _____. Although Freud believed that attachment grew out of a mother's meeting her child's _____ needs, _____ work with infant monkeys disproved this: his infant monkeys preferred _____ mothers over those who fed them. Bowlby believed that attachment was based upon the infant's need for _____.

The _____ Strange Situation is based upon the Bowlby model. Infants tend to behave in one of _____ ways in this test. Most American infants are _____ attached. _____ children, in contrast, _____ their mothers, while _____ children exhibit a combination of _____ and _____ behaviors towards their mothers. The least well-attached children are described as disorganized - _____. Quality of attachment appears to have _____ effects on a person's behavior.

At the same time, there are _____ differences in attachment patterns. Secure attachments are most common in those cultures that favor _____.

Mothers of securely attached infants are appropriately _____ to their infants' needs. Some infant characteristics that might contribute to attachment are _____ and emotional _____; the data are at this point _____. An infant's attachment to her mother and her father tends to be _____. This is in part because fathers spend relatively more time _____ with their infants and less time _____ for them. Fathers also play more _____ with their infants.

Infants and parents _____ determine the pace and nature of their interactions; they _____ regulate each other.

Infants are _____ in each other, and, generally, they become _____ sociable as they get older. They play simple _____ with each other and _____ each other's behavior. They even _____ each other new behaviors.

Differences Among Infants

From birth onwards, infants have enduring _____ traits.
_____ identified two infant traits that he believed would
endure throughout a person's entire life. Erikson's first crisis involves _____ vs. _____; it lasts from birth to
_____ months of age. Children become optimistic if
their caretakers _____ meet their needs. Towards the end
of infancy, babies develop a sense of _____; if they do
not, they feel shame and _____. To encourage this positive sense, parents should encourage _____ and avoid
being _____.

personality (207)
Erikson (207)

trust; mistrust (207)
12 (207)
consistently (207)
autonomy (207)
doubt (207)
exploration (207)
overprotective (207)

Temperament refers to _____ children behave. These
differences are present at _____ and are largely _____.
These traits are stable through at least _____.
Temperament is composed of _____ traits including
_____ level and _____.

how (207)
birth (207); innate (207)
adolescence (207)
9 (207);
activity (207); irritability (208)

_____ babies have a positive disposition: they are regular
and _____. _____ of babies fall into this category.
_____ babies are more negative, and are _____ to
adapt. About _____ of babies fit into this category.
Finally, about _____ of babies are _____: they are
_____ and initially cautious of new situations. About
_____ of babies cannot be categorized.

Easy (208)
adaptable (208); 40% (208)
Difficult (208); slow (208) 10%
(208)
15% (208); slow to warm
(208); inactive (208)
35% (208)

What matters most is not what temperament a baby has, but
rather its _____ with the child's environment.

goodness of fit (209)

Parents encourage _____ differences. Girls and boys are
_____ with differently and their behaviors are _____
differently. While there do appear to be _____ innate differences between boys and girls, these differences _____
as children age. For example, by age 2 boys are more
_____ and less _____ than girls.

gender (209)
played (209); interpreted (209)
minor (210)
increase (210)

independent (210); compliant
(210)

The American family has changed greatly during the past
40 years. The number of _____ families has greatly
increased, and at the same time the average family size has
_____. More and more children are being born to
_____, often _____ mothers. In the 1990s, _____ of
American children live in _____.

single-parent (211)

shrunk (210)
unmarried (212); adolescent
(212); 25% (212); poverty
(212)

employed (212); does not (212)

advantages (212)

securely (213)

trained (215); 3 or 4 (214)
play with (215)
clean (215)

Many children must attend day care because their parents are _____. High-quality day care _____ appear to be harmful to children. In fact, many studies have shown clear _____ to high-quality day-care attendance. Some studies, though, have indicated problems. In particular, some studies have shown that children who attended day care as infants were less likely to be _____ attached.

Day-care centers vary widely in quality. High-quality centers have one _____ adult for every _____ infants, and these adults _____ the children. High quality centers are also safe and _____.

Crossword Puzzle

Social and Personality Development in Infancy

Across

1 _____ socialization: infants and caregivers influence each other

3 About 2/3 of children are _____ attached.

5 _____-of-fit

8 _____ children do not seek proximity to their caretakers.

10 The _____ regulation model of emotional communication

11 _____ vs. shame and doubt

13 _____ smiles are smiles in response to others

14 A theory of _____ is a child's beliefs about the mental world.

16 _____ babies often have negative moods.

17 An emotional response corresponding to the emotions of another

18 Social _____ occurs when you use others for information.

20 Disorganized-_____ children

21 Self-_____ is one's knowledge of oneself.

22 Patterns of arousal and emotionality present at birth

23 _____ children get angry with their mothers after they have been reunited.

25 The founder of the theory of psychosocial development

Down

2 _____ theory: its first stage is trust vs. mistrust

4 The sense of being male or female

6 _____ anxiety: the distress infants feel when a caretaker leaves them

7 Slow-to-_____ babies don't like new situations.

9 _____ anxiety: the wariness displayed by infants when they meet a new person

12 The positive emotional bond between a child and another

15 The total sum of a person's enduring characteristics

16 _____ emotions theory

19 The _____ Strange Situation Test

24 _____ babies have a positive disposition.

Flash Cards

What evidence could be used to support the idea that emotional expression is innate?	What causes stranger anxiety?
What factors influence the amount of stranger anxiety an infant exhibits?	How does smiling change during infancy?
Give an example of social referencing.	How does social referencing work?
How is infant self-recognition tested?	What are "compliant agents"?
What are two differences between attachment and imprinting?	Describe the Strange Situation.

Cognitive development allows infants to distinguish familiar from unknown persons	Infants all over the world display the same emotions in the same way.
The youngest infants only smile reflexively; next infants smile at anything that interests them; finally they smile only to those things or people they truly like.	Infants who are frequently exposed to strangers exhibit less; infants react less strongly to women and children than to male adults.
We don't know. It could be that infants get an empathic response or it might be that they simply use the other's reaction as information.	An infant who is approached by a stranger will glance at her mother to see her mother's reaction. If the mother is positive, so too will be the baby.
Other people, who behave intentionally and have the potential to comply with an infant's requests.	With the mirror and rouge task; a dab of rouge is placed on an infant's nose. If the infant touches his own nose after looking in the mirror, he is self-aware.
Mother and child enter an unfamiliar room. The mother sits and waits. An experimenter enters and the mother leaves. She returns and the stranger leaves.	Imprinting is instantaneous; attachments develop slowly. Imprinting is clearly innate; attachment is partially influenced by the environment.

Why are securely attached infants called "secure" when they are afraid and upset when their mothers leave them?

Give a specific example of a cultural difference in attachment pattern.

Name the four different attachment patterns

How do mothers of insecurely attached infants behave?

Give an example of how infant temperament might influence attachment?

According to Erikson, what determines what kinds of personalities an infant will develop?

What factors contribute to infants' temperaments, and which is most important?

Name at least five dimensions of temperament.

Give an example of goodness of fit for temperament.

Contrast the terms "sex" and "gender."

Give several examples of neonatal behavioral gender differences that are probably innate.

Name some of the positive effects of high-quality day care on infants.

German children are more likely to be avoidantly attached than American children.	Because they use their mothers as secure bases from which to explore their surroundings
They ignore their babies' signals, they behave inconsistently with them, and they ignore or reject them.	Securely attached, avoidantly attached, ambivalently attached, and disorganized-disoriented attachments
The kind of care his or her parents provide	It is easier to consistently care for a baby who is regular and predictable than one who is not.
Activity level, irritability, rhythmicity, intensity, general mood, and approach/withdrawal	Heredity (most important), the prenatal environment, and the child's birth experience
"Sex" refers to one's anatomy; "gender" refers to the role requirements of masculinity/ femininity as defined by one's culture.	A calm, inactive child might not be appreciated by intense, energetic parents (even though other parents might be very pleased).
Infants who have attended high quality day care are more sociable and cooperative.	Male neonates are more active, fussier, and more irritable than female neonates.

Name some of the negative effects
that have been found in infants
attending day care.

Some studies have found them less
likely to be securely attached, and
also to be more aggressive.

Practice Test One

1. Most psychologists believe that
   a. infants cannot express emotions.
   b. infants may seem to express emotions, but they are not really feeling them.
   c. infants feel many emotions, but cannot express them.
   d. infants can express and actually experience a number of basic emotions.

2. Which of the following is a true difference between stranger and separation anxiety?
   a. Infants do not express distress when they experience stranger anxiety.
   b. Separation anxiety begins a little later than stranger anxiety.
   c. Only females (strangers or caretakers) can trigger stranger and separation anxiety.
   d. Stranger and separation anxiety levels are surprisingly consistent among infants.

3. Infants' earliest smiles are
   a. reflexes.
   b. in response to the human voice.
   c. in response to familiar faces.
   d. highly selective.

4. Tory's mother is very tired and so is just sitting there without moving and with a blank look on her face. Tory, who is 18 months old, will
   a. smile and attempt to engage her mother in play.
   b. become distressed.
   c. get angry at her mother.
   d. ignore her mother.

5. Two-year-old Amol and his parents are picnicking in the park. An inquisitive squirrel leaps onto their blanket. Amol's mother freezes while Amol's father laughs. Amol will most likely
   a. imitate his father and laugh.
   b. imitate his mother and freeze.
   c. try to both laugh and freeze at the same time.
   d. become distressed because he is receiving conflicting signals.

6. Newborn infants
   a. are not self-aware.
   b. cannot imitate other people's facial expressions.
   c. are incapable of expressing any emotions.
   d. all of the above are true

7. The fact that 2-year olds try to relieve others' distress indicates that
   a. they have self-awareness.
   b. they can encode emotions.
   c. they are to some degree empathic.
   d. they are capable of social referencing.

8. Harlow's work proved that
   a. human attachments are innate and hard-wired.
   b. human infants bond almost instantaneously with their mothers after birth.
   c. secure attachments are the best.
   d. attachment is in good part based upon contact comfort.

9. Which of the following is not a form of attachment?
   a. inconsistent
   b. ambivalent
   c. disorganized-disoriented
   d. avoidant

10. What cultural value tends to promote secure attachments in infants?
    a. obedience
    b. independence
    c. nurturance
    d. empathy

11. Which of the following statements is true?
    a. The majority of American fathers do almost no child care.
    b. Fathers play more gently with their children than do mothers.
    c. American fathers treat their infants quite differently than fathers in many different cultures.
    d. Fathers spend a greater portion of the time they spend with their infants playing than mothers.

12. Which of the following statements is true?
    a. Parents consistently have more influence over turn-taking than infants.
    b. Infants consistently have more influence over turn-taking than parents.
    c. Infant control of turn-taking steadily increases as they get older.
    d. During most of infancy, parent and child have equal control over turn-taking.

13. Infants
    a. tend to ignore each other.
    b. form true friendships with each other.
    c. often act aggressively towards each other.
    d. play simple games and enjoy each other.

14. The first Eriksonian life stage involves
    a. autonomy.
    b. curiosity.
    c. attachment.
    d. trust.

15. Terry is a rather inactive baby: he generally lies quietly and gazes rather than crawls. When confronted with a new situation, such as a new toy, he most often turns away from it or pushes it away. Terry would be described as a(n)
    a. easy baby.
    b. passive baby.
    c. slow-to-warm baby.
    d. difficult baby.

16. Gender differences between boys and girls tend to
    a. begin during late infancy.
    b. begin after infancy.
    c. decrease during infancy.
    d. increase during infancy.

17. Which of the following is not currently true of American families?
    a. People are choosing to have more children than before.
    b. There are more unwed mothers than in previous generations.
    c. More children will live in a one-parent home than in the past.
    d. Approximately 25% of American children are poor.

18. Which children are most at risk if placed into day care during infancy?
    a. Middle-class children who have two working parents.
    b. High risk poor children who have secure attachments with their mothers.
    c. High risk children who have insecure attachments to their fathers.
    d. Girls

19. High-quality day care centers
    a. are usually large.
    b. have one teacher for every 3 or 4 infants.
    c. have high staff turn-over rates.
    d. all of the above

Test Solutions

Self-Quiz Solution

1. d (page 191)
2. b (page 192)
3. a (page 192)
4. b (page 193)
5. d (page 194)
6. a (page 194)
7. c (page 195)
8. d (page 197)
9. a (page198)
10. b (page(200)

11. d (page202)
12. d (page203)
13. d (page204)
14. d (page 207)
15. c (page208)
16. d (page210)
17. a (page211)
18. b (page213)
19. b (page 214)

Crossword Puzzle Solution

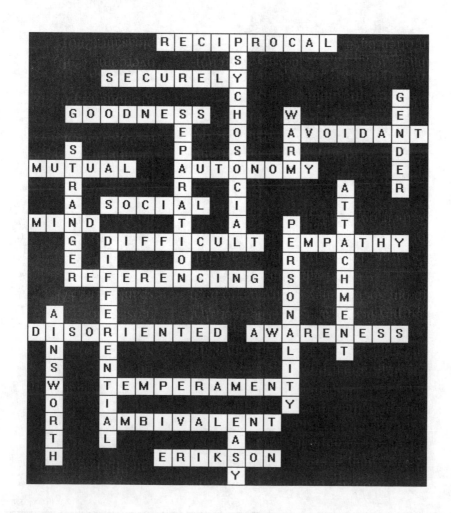

CHAPTER 7

Physical Development in the Preschool Years

INTERESTING AND IMPORTANT THINGS YOU'LL KNOW AFTER READING THIS CHAPTER...

1. Are girls' and boys' brains different? See page 227.

2. What is the most common sleep disorder in young children? See page 229.

3. What is the most serious health hazard facing America's preschoolers? See page 234.

Learning Objectives

When you have mastered the material in this chapter, you should be able to ...

1. Describe the change in physical proportions, height, and weight that occur during the preschool years. (page 224)

2. Discuss the rapid development of the brain and nervous system. (page 226)

3. Understand the role that gender and culture might play in brain development and lateralization. (page 227)

4. List advances in sensory and perceptual development that occur between 3 and 6 years of age. (page 228)

5. Describe the major sleep disorders that affect preschoolers. (page 229)

6. Explain how preschoolers' nutritional needs change and how to help them avoid obesity. (page 230)

7. Describe the most frequent major and minor illnesses contracted by preschoolers. (page 231)

8. Discuss preschoolers' risk from accidents, poisonings, and physical injuries. (page 233)

9. Contrast physical abuse, psychological maltreatment and neglect, understanding who abuses, and who is most likely to be abused. (page 236)

10. Understand the characteristics that make some children particularly resilient and resistant to the effects of a poor environment. (page 240)

11. Describe the advancements in gross motor skills that occur during the preschool years. (page 241)

12. Explain the nature and causes of gender differences in gross motor skills in 3- to 6-year olds. (page 242)

13. List several fine motor accomplishments made during this stage of life. (page 243)

14. Discuss the development of handedness. (page 243)

15. Outline the development of artistic ability in preschool-age children. (page 244)

16. Cite several strategies to help keep preschoolers healthy. (page 245)

Guided Review

Physical Growth

At the end of infancy, the average American child is _____ inches tall and weighs _____ pounds. By the end of the preschool period, American children average _____ inches and weigh _____ pounds. During this time span, gender differences in height and weight _____. Children who are malnourished are _____ than children who are not.

36 (224)
25-30 (224)
46 (224)
46 (224)
increase (224)
smaller (225)

Preschoolers' _____ change as well. Children tend to become more _____ during these years, and their arms and legs _____. Children mature _____ as well.

proportions (225)
slender (225)
lengthen (226); internally (226)

The _____ is the fastest growing organ in the body. It grows because neural _____ become more numerous and more _____ is produced. Lateralization proceeds, which means that its two halves become more _____. In most people, the left hemisphere concentrates upon _____ skills while the right specializes in _____ expression and _____ relationships. The two hemispheres remain _____, however.

brain (226)
interconnections (226)
myelin (226)
specialized (226)
language (226)
emotional (226)
spatial (226)
interdependent (227)

There appear to be _____ differences in brain functioning. In particular, language is _____ localized in boys' _____ hemispheres than in girls'. In addition, a part of the _____ is larger in girls than in boys. These differences may be due to _____ or to different _____. In addition, there is some evidence that _____ can affect lateralization.

gender (227)
more (227)
left (227)
corpus collosum (227);
genes (227); stimulation (227)
culture (227)

As the brain improves, so do the _____. Visual _____ becomes more adult-like. Preschoolers become progressively better at looking at _____ rather than at _____ of stimuli.

senses (228); scanning (228)

whole objects (228); parts (228)

Approximately _____ of preschoolers have trouble falling asleep. Vivid bad dreams, or _____, usually occur early in the morning. More severe are night _____, which occur in approximate _____ of children. The most common sleep disorder, however, is _____. Most children spontaneously outgrow this problem or can be helped with an _____ or by use of _____.

20%-30% (229)
nightmares (229)
terrors (229)
1%-5% (229)
enuresis (229)

alarm device (229); reward (229)

healthy (230)

accidents (230)

less (231)
successful (231)
obese (231)

closer (231)
Environmental (231)

internal (231)
push (231)
restrictions (231)
variety (231);
fat (231)
iron (231)

colds (231)

benefits (231)

vaccines (232); Low-income
(231)
supervaccine (232)
one (232)

leukemia (233); cancer (233);
white (233)
70% (233)
AIDS (233); fatal (233)
delays (233)

difficult (233)

three (233)
Boys (234)
risks (234)
active (234); poisons (235)
car seats (235)

water (235)

The majority of American preschoolers are quite _____. In this country, children's health is most often threatened by _____.

Preschoolers generally eat _____ than infants. Although most children are _____ at regulating their food intake, some children become _____ by over eating. This condition is in part genetic: for example, adopted children's weights are usually _____ to their biological parents' weights rather than their adopted parents'. _____ factors also contribute greatly to preschooler weight. Children need to learn to develop _____ controls on eating, and both parents who _____ children to eat or who place strong _____ on their eating are doing a disservice to their children. The best strategy is for parents to provide a _____ of high nutrition, low _____ foods during the day. In particular, they should provide a diet with plenty of _____.

The average preschooler has 7 or 8 _____ from age 3 to 5. Although unpleasant, researchers now think that there are _____ to these minor illnesses.

Most American preschoolers do not get serious illnesses due to the availability of _____. _____ US children and children in the Third World are not so fortunate. Researchers are searching for a _____ which would allow children to become immunized after just _____ oral dose.

The most frequent serious illness to strike preschoolers is _____, a form of _____ in which the bone marrow produces too many _____ blood cells. Fortunately, more than _____ of sufferers can now be cured. This is not true of pediatric _____, an ultimately _____ disease in children that causes developmental _____. Most preschoolers who must spend time in the hospital find the experience very _____.

Every year, one in _____ American children has an injury requiring medical attention. _____ are particularly likely to be injured, because they like taking _____ and are physically _____. Parents should lock _____ away, make sure that their children use _____ when traveling, and never leave children unattended when they are in _____.

Physical Development in the Preschool Years

_____ children, whose environments are filled with more hazards, are also at special risk of injury. In particular, they are vulnerable to _____ poisoning. Exposure to this substance can lead to lower _____, _____ and increased _____. It can even cause _____.

Low-income (235)

lead (234)
intelligence (234); hyperactivity (234); aggression (234)
death (235)

Child abuse is more common than most people realize: annually more than _____ US children are abused. _____ abuse — e.g., beating or burning a child — occurs most often in households with high _____ levels. Preschoolers, especially _____ preschoolers, are among the _____ likely to be physically abused. The fact that _____ is acceptable in our society may contribute to high abuse rates, as is the _____ with which many of us raise our children. People who were themselves abused as children are _____ likely to be abusive than other parents, but most _____ abuse their own children.

3 million (236)
Physical (236)
stress (236)
fussy (236)
most (236)
spanking (237)
privacy (237)

more (238)
do not (238)

Parents can harm children _____ as well, by frightening, _____, or humiliating them. In cases of _____, parents ignore their children. Although some children are _____, many children who have suffered from psychological abuse have severe, _____ effects.

psychologically (238)
intimidating (238); neglect (239); resilient (239)

life-long (239)

Resilient children manage to _____ adverse circumstances. These children often have _____ temperaments and evoke _____ from those around them. They tend to be _____ and _____ and to feel in _____.

overcome (240)
pleasant (240)
care (240)
intelligent (240); outgoing (240); control (240)

Motor Development

_____ motor skills — those involving large areas of the body — develop rapidly during preschool. Three-year olds can _____, hop, skip, and _____. Four-year olds can _____ accurately. Five-year olds can ride _____.

Gross (241)

jump (241); run (241)
throw (241); a bike (241)

_____ levels are extremely high during this stage of life. There are, of course, _____ in these levels.

Activity (241)
individual differences (241)

Boys' gross motor skills surpass girls' in some ways: they are _____, _____ better and jump higher. They are also more _____ than girls. Conversely, girls are better at coordinating their _____ and _____. Some of these differences are due to _____ and some due to _____.

stronger (242); throw (242); active (242)
arms (242); legs (242)
heredity (242); environment (242)

fine (243)
puzzles (243)
pencil (243)

7 months (243)
preschool (243); 90% (243);
is not (243)

art (244); planning (244);
restraint (244)
scribbling (244); shapes (244)
designs (244)

pictorial (244); 5 (244)

well-balanced (245)
5 to 7 (245)

sleep (245); wash (245)
vaccines (245)

More delicate _____ motor skills are also developing. By three, children can complete simple _____; by five, they can hold and use a _____.

Some children begin to show a preference for one hand as early as _____; most favor one hand by the end of _____. About _____ of children are right-handed. It _____ intrinsically bad to be left-handed; however, most people are right-handed, everyday tools are designed with the right-handed in mind.

As their fine motor skills improve, young children become more adept at _____. This teaches them _____ and self-_____. The first step in the development of drawing is _____. By three, children are making _____; they then begin to combine these forms into _____. When they begin to draw recognizable objects, they have moved into the _____ stage. This occurs at about _____ years of age.

Concerned parents who wish to keep their preschoolers as healthy as possible should feed them _____ diets; preferably children of this age should be fed _____ times per day. Parents should insist that their children get enough _____. Children should _____ their hands to cut down on illness rates, and receive all of their needed _____ on time.

Crossword Puzzle

Physical Development In the Preschool Years

Across

2   A state of being more than 20% overweight

4   Cycle-of-_____

6   Night _____: a state of intense physiological arousal that awakens a child in a state of panic.

11 The state in which certain functions are carried out more by one of the brain's hemispheres

13 Corpus _____

Down

1   Protective insulation around a neuron

3   A child's first drawings

5   A vivid, bad dream

7   The ability to overcome adverse circumstances

8   A preference for the use of one hand

9   Ignoring a child's needs

10 A lack of bladder control

12 The physical or psychological maltreatment of a child

Flash Cards

Describe how preschoolers' proportions change.

Describe an internal change in the ear that occurs during the preschool years.

Describe the difference in the way that the brains of boys and girls process language.

How does visual scanning change during preschool?

How might preschoolers' hearing abilities help account for their distractibility?

Contrast nightmares and night terrors.

What are the three major contributors to poor health in children?

Give a piece of evidence suggesting that obesity is in part genetic.

What kinds of food should parents provide for their preschoolers?

What kinds of foods are rich in iron?

The Eustacian tube, which connects the throat with the middle ear, becomes more vertical.

Preschoolers lose body fat and their pot bellies, their arms and legs lengthen, and their heads become relatively smaller than infants'.

Two- and 3-year olds scan the interiors of shapes; 4- and 5-year olds scan the edges; 6- and 7-year olds look around the outsides of objects.

Boys process language almost solely in their left hemispheres; girls process language more equally in both.

Nightmares are remembered; night terrors are not. Nightmares are quite common; night terrors are not.

Preschoolers are not adept at separating out simultaneously presented sounds.

Children's weights are most similar to their biological, not adoptive parents', and as babies obese individuals had a sweet tooth.

Illness, malnutrition, and physical injury

Red meats, dark green vegetables, and whole grains.

They should provide foods low in fat and high in iron and other nutrients.

What four benefits do children get out of having colds?

What is happening to the US immunization rate and why?

What will make a vaccine a "supervaccine?"

How many children around the world die from infectious diseases each year?

What are some of the major infectious diseases that strike children for which there are vaccines?

In addition to the physical consequences of their illness, what other problems face children with AIDS?

What interventions can help children cope with being hospitalized?

List some of the most common causes of childhood accidental injury.

How does lead affect children?

Why are lower-income children more at risk for lead poisoning?

What can parents do to decrease the risk of lead poisoning for their children?

Describe the home environments most associated with physical abuse.

It has been falling, probably due to a lack of a national health care policy.

(1) Build up immunities; (2) learn about their bodies; (3) learn coping skills; (4) become more empathic

About 2 million

It will vaccinate against all major illnesses in one oral dose and would not need refrigeration.

(1) They are shunned by others. (2) Their families are frequently disrupted.

Measles, influenza, polio, tetanus, diphtheria, tuberculosis

Falls, burns, drowning, suffocation, car accidents, and poisonings

Permitting their parents to stay with them, or assigning one special nurse to nurture them

They live in older homes with peeling, lead-based paint. Inner-city children breathe more air pollution.

Lead poisoning can lead to loss of intelligence, processing problems, hyperactivity, distractibility, aggression or death.

Lower income; single-parent; marital conflict; families with step-parents; families in which the parent had been abused

They can make their children wash their hands more, keep their children's nails short, remove old paint and provide a good diet.

At what ages are children most vulnerable to physical abuse?

How do experts feel about the practice of spanking children for misbehavior?

List four factors that contribute to high American physical abuse rates.

Describe the consequences of psychological maltreatment.

What is it about resilient children that lets them succeed?

Why does motor skill improve so rapidly during the preschool years?

Give a piece of evidence which suggests that activity levels are in part genetic.

List one way that boys' motor skills outstrip girls'; list one way that girls' motor development outstrips boys'.

Why do boys get more practice in doing gross motor movements than girls?

Why are lefties more likely to die at an early age than righties?

What benefits — other than aesthetic ones — do children get from drawing and producing art?

List the four stages of the development of drawing in the correct sequence.

They are almost unanimously against it.	Between 3 and 4, and between 15 to 17 years of age
Low self-esteem, lying, poor conduct, underachievement; aggression, depression, suicide	(1) Tolerance of spanking (2) privacy (3) insensitivity to age norms (4) cycle-of-violence
Brain development and myelinization make motor development possible; high activity/practice levels also contribute.	They *evoke* care from others, they are intelligent, they are independent and feel in control of their destinies.
Boys are stronger than girls; girls can coordinate their arms and legs better than boys.	Monozygotic twins have more similar activity levels than dizygotic twins.
Because most devices are built for ease of use with the right hand, lefties are more accident-prone than righties.	Boys play activities involve more gross motor activity than girls', and so they get more practice.
(1) Scribbling; (2) shapes (3) design (4) pictorial	They practice their fine motor skills, learn to plan, learn restraint, and learn self-correction.

How many calories should the
average preschooler consume
each day?

About 1300 when they are three
and 1700 when they are five

Practice Test One

1. Children reach half their adult height when they are about
   a. 2 years old.
   b. 3 years old.
   c. 5 years old.
   d. 6 years old.

2. What is the function of myelin?
   a. It increases lateralization.
   b. It enhances sensory ability.
   c. It speeds up neural transmission.
   d. It produces new interconnections in the brain.

3. Which part of the brain is larger in girls than in boys?
   a. the left hemisphere
   b. the right hemisphere
   c. the hippocampus
   d. the corpus collosum

4. What sensory advance helps children to read when they are about six?
   a. auditory acuity
   b. the ability to scan shapes effectively
   c. increased intermodal sensory transfer
   d. increased sensitivity to contrast

5. Why is enuresis a problem?
   a. It frequently indicates an underlying physical problem.
   b. It frequently is a symptom of an underlying psychological problem.
   c. It tends to worsen as children age.
   d. It can cause a child shame and embarrassment.

6. Tyrone, who used to have a large appetite when he was an infant, has become a fussy eater at three. He often picks at his food, and some days seems to eat hardly at all. Tyrone's parents should
   a. strongly encourage him to eat more.
   b. provide his favorite foods, even if they are less nutritious than others.
   c. let him as eat as much as he wants.
   d. praise him for his lowered intake and warn him of the risks of over-eating.

7. The most common major illness in preschool children is
   a. leukemia.
   b. pediatric AIDS.
   c. encephalitis.
   d. diabetes.

8. The most serious health threat to young children in this country is
   a. influenza.
   b. lead poisoning.
   c. car accidents.
   d. pediatric AIDS.

9. Marta was an unwanted child, a result of an unplanned pregnancy — a fact of which they frequently remind her. They tell her she is stupid and worthless, and that their lives would have been better had she never been born. Marta is at great risk of
   a. developing low self-esteem.
   b. underachieving in school.
   c. becoming a chronic liar.
   d. all of the above

10. Which of the following traits is *not* particularly characteristic of resilient children?
    a. being loners
    b. being intelligent
    c. being easy-going
    d. having feelings of control

11. Which of the following gross motor abilities can a typical 3-year old perform?
    a. ride a bicycle
    b. climb a ladder
    c. hop on one foot
    d. throw a ball fairly accurately

12. Which of the following statements is false?
    a. Preschool-aged boys are more coordinated than preschool-aged girls.
    b. Preschool boys are stronger than preschool girls.
    c. Preschool boys are more physically active than preschool girls.
    d. None of the above statements is false.

13. John is 4 1/5 years old. Which of the following can he probably not yet do?
    a. hold and draw with a pencil
    c. put simple jigsaw puzzles together
    b. fold paper into triangles
    d. undo his clothes

14. The best scientific evidence suggests that left-handed persons
    a. are less intelligent, as a whole, than right-handed persons.
    b. are more physically frail and illness prone than right-handed. persons.
    c. should be taught to use their right hands as much as possible.
    d. are not intrinsically worse off than right-handed persons

15. The stage at which children begin to draw recognizable objects is called the
    a. the design stage.
    b. scribbling.
    c. the pictorial stage.
    d. the shape stage.

16. Why do preschoolers need to eat so frequently?
    a. They need a very large number of calories.
    b. They dehydrate easily.
    c. Their stomachs are small.
    d. They cannot yet digest food as easily as adults.

Test Solutions

Self-Quiz Solution

1. a (page 224)
2. c (page 226)
3. d (page 227)
4. b (page 228)
5. d (page 229)
6. c (page 231)
7. a (page 233)
8. b (page 234)

9. d (page 239)
10. a (page 240)
11. c (page 241)
12. a (page 242)
13. a (page 243)
14. d (page 243)
15. c (page 244)
16. c (page 245)

Crossword Puzzle Solution

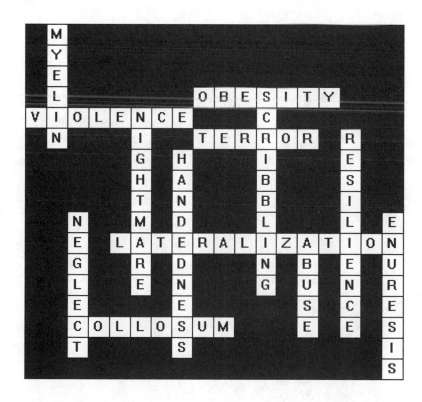

CHAPTER 8

Cognitive Development in the Preschool Years

INTERESTING AND IMPORTANT THINGS YOU'LL KNOW AFTER READING THIS CHAPTER...

Learning Objectives

When you have mastered the material in this chapter, you should be able to ...

1. Describe the major features of preoperational thought. (page 252)

2. Give examples of conservation problems, and know what cognitive skills are needed to solve them. (page 256)

3. Critique the Piagetian approach to preschooler cognitive ability. (page 257)

4. Discuss preschoolers' autobiographical memory. (page 259)

5. Describe the relationship between musical training and the development of spatial skills. (page 260)

6. Explain Lev Vygotsky's view of cognitive development. (page 261)

7. Outline the improvements in syntax, grammar, and pragmatics that occur during the preschool years. (page 263)

8. Contrast children's use of private speech and social speech. (page 265)

9. Discuss how socioeconomic status affects children's language acquisition. (page 266)

10. Contrast the available options of preschool out-of-home educational care. (page 268)

11. Describe how children who attend preschool compare academically and socially to children who stay at home. (page 269)

12. Compare the American preschool situation with that in several European countries and understand why our situation is different. (page 270)

13. Explain the purpose of Head Start programs and be aware of their degree of success. (page 272)

14. Describe the magnitude of television in preschoolers' lives and discuss how well children understand what they view on television. (page 275)

15. Discuss the effects that watching educational programs such as *Sesame Street* has on preschoolers. (page 275)

16. List several ways that parents and teachers can work to promote preschoolers' cognitive development. (page 277)

Guided Review

Intellectual Development

According to Piaget, preschoolers are in the _____ stage of cognitive development, which lasts from _____ years of age. During this time, children's reasoning becomes more _____ and they have less of a need to physically _____ on objects in order to understand them. They remain incapable of performing mental _____, however. Because they can use symbols, their ability to use _____ increases dramatically. In general, Piaget _____ preschoolers' cognitive skills.

preoperational (252)
2 to 7 (252)

symbolic (252)
act (252)
operations (252)
language (252)
underestimated (252)

Piaget believed that language and thinking are _____. Once they enter the preoperational period, children think more _____ than before, their thinking is not so tied to the _____, and they can think about several things _____.

intertwined (253)

quickly (253)
present (253); simultaneously (253)

The main limitation of preoperational thinking is _____. Generally preschoolers focus only upon a _____, obvious, _____ aspect of a stimulus. To a preschooler, _____ is everything.

centration (253)
single (253)
external (253); appearance (253)

A second limitation of preoperational thought is _____, an inability to takes another's _____. Preschoolers are not _____ but they do not realize that others have different _____.

egocentrism (254)
viewpoint (254)
selfish (254)
perspectives (254)

Preschoolers also have difficulty in understanding _____, especially their _____ steps.

transformations (254)
intermediate (254)

During preoperations, preschoolers develop _____ thought and become intensely _____. They often believe that they _____ more than they really do. At this time they begin to understand the concept of _____; that is, they know that actions and outcomes are related to each other. By the end of preoperations, they begin to understand _____ and know that things can change appearance. By the end of the preoperational period, they can solve _____ problems.

intuitive (255)
curious (255)
know (255)
functionality (256)

identity (256)
conservation (256)

number (257)

continuous (257)
earlier (257)

competencies (259)
autobiographical (259)
fade (259)
distorted (259)
scripts (259)

4 (260)
compare (260)

music (260); spatial (260)

Vygotsky (261); social (261)

jointly (261)

proximal (262)
almost (262)
scaffolding (262)

rapidly (263)
length (263); syntax (263)
14,000 (263)

mapping (263); plurals (263)
articles (263)
past tense (263)

rules (264); Most (264)

pragmatics (264)

Piaget's views are not all accepted today. For example, preschoolers have a better understanding of _____ than he thought. Most developmental psychologists believe that their cognitive development is more _____ than he imagined. Conservation develops somewhat _____ than he believed.

Information processors have focused more upon preschoolers' cognitive _____ than their deficiencies. One aspect of cognition that they have studied is _____ memory. Most of these memories _____ over time, and those that last can be _____. Preschoolers usually remember their routines by using _____, and cannot really distinguish one day's events from another's.

By _____ years of age, most preschoolers can do simple addition problems, and they can _____ different quantities successfully.

Information processors have also suggested that giving children _____ lessons increases their _____ abilities.

Yet another approach to cognitive development was proposed by Lev _____. He emphasized the _____ aspects of learning. He believed that children become smarter when they work _____ with others to solve problems. Vygotsky believed that the most useful types of problems are those which fall into a child's zone of _____ development, the level at which a child can _____ solve a problem on his or her own. The best teachers employ _____, and encourage children to cognitively grow.

The Growth of Language

Language develops _____ during the preschool years. Sentence _____ increases steadily, and _____ becomes more complex. By 6, most children have _____-word vocabularies, a feat they manage by a process called fast _____. Three-year olds can correctly use _____ and _____ such as "a" and "the". They put sentences in the _____ by adding "ed" to the end of verbs. It is clear that they are not merely repeating what they have heard, but are mastering the underlying _____ of language. _____ of what preschoolers say is grammatically correct. Children also master _____, and understand the social conventions of speech.

Preschoolers frequently engage in _____ speech. As they get older, they may begin to _____ such speech or merely _____ their lips. This speech helps children _____ and helps them _____ their own behavior. Piaget, who believed that such speech was _____ and egocentric, was likely wrong. As children get older, more and more of their speech is _____.

private (265)
whisper (265)
move (265); think (265)
control (265)
immature (265)

social (265)

Wealthier parents spend _____ time speaking to their children than do lower-income parents, and they are less likely to issue _____ when speaking. This is significant because there is a correlation between language exposure and _____.

more (266)

prohibitions (266)

intelligence (267)

Schooling and Society

Almost _____ of American children attend some form of preschool. Many attend because their mothers are _____ and there is no one home to care for them. _____ American children less than 7 years of age are in this situation.

3/4 (268)

employed (268)
Most (268)

Early education takes several forms. _____ centers usually provide _____ care for children. Their primary emphasis is typically _____ rather than _____. Some programs are run out of private _____: these centers are often not _____, and their quality is _____.

Day-care (268)
all-day (268)
social (268); cognitive (268)
homes (268)
licensed (268); variable (268)

Preschools, or _____ schools, are more geared towards _____ experiences; children typically attend between _____ hours per day, and are largely from _____ socioeconomic homes. Finally, _____ day care is provided by some local school systems. These programs are usually targeted at _____ children and are often of _____ quality.

nursery (269)
cognitive (269)
3 and 5 (269); middle and
upper (269); school (269)

disadvantaged (269); high
(269)

High-quality preschool programs are _____ to children both _____ and _____. _____ children are especially benefited. However, some studies have shown that there are costs to attending as well: children who have attended out-of-home programs are less _____ and more _____ than their peers.

beneficial (269)
socially (269); cognitively
(269); Underprivileged (269)

polite (270); competitive (270)

poor (270)
do not (271)
do not (271)

less (271)

Head Start (273)
has been (273)

social (273); held back (273)
intelligence (273)

20 (274); 30 (274)
do not (275)

plot (275)
fantasy (275)
motivations (275)
not representative (275)

Sesame Street (275)
vocabularies (275)
reading (276)
no evidence (276)

just above (277)

individualized (277); pace (277)
social (277)
too hard (277)

Much American preschool education is of _____ quality. We _____ have a national policy on preschool education, and we _____ have a history of formally teaching preschoolers. Furthermore, we pay preschool teachers _____ than other teachers.

_____ is a preschool program designed to help disadvantaged children. It _____ successful at preparing children for kindergarten, and graduates are less likely to have _____ problems in school or to be _____. It does not, however, produce long-term advances in _____.

The average preschooler spends between _____ and _____ hours per week watching television. They _____ fully understand what they watch, however. Preschoolers frequently fail to understand a show's _____, and they cannot distinguish between _____ and reality. They do not understand the characters' _____. Another problem is that much of what they view is _____ of the real world.

Still, there can be benefits to viewing. Shows such as _____ are beneficial to preschoolers. For example, children who watch the show have larger _____ than those who do not and they spend more time _____. There is _____ that watching this show decreases interest and enjoyment in traditional schooling.

The best way to foster intellectual growth in preschoolers is to give them cognitive tasks that are _____ their level of functioning. (This implies that instruction should be _____.) Students should be allowed to _____ themselves and _____ opportunities should be provided. Preschoolers should not be pushed _____.

Crossword Puzzle

Cognitive Development During the Preschool Years

Across

1 Lev _____

5 A synonym for "nursery schools"

8 _____ centers are places that provide all-day care for children while their parents are at work.

9 Organized, formal, logical mental processes

13 Zone of _____ Development

15 _____ speech is directed towards other persons.

18 Fast _____

21 Head _____

22 _____ memory is one's memory for one's own life and past.

Down

2 _____ function: the ability to use a word or an object to represent something not present

3 When one focuses on one limited aspect of a stimulus and ignores others

4 _____ speech is not intended for others and helps individuals think.

6 The combining of words or phrases to form sentences

7 The aspect of language relating to communicating effectively with others

8 _____ appropriate educational practice

10 The _____ stage of cognitive development lasts from 2 until 7.

11 The process by which one state is changed into another

12 The knowledge that quantity is not related to objects' physical appearance

14 The support for learning that encourages independence and growth

16 Describes the thinking of preschoolers that fails to take others' perspectives into account

17 _____ reflects preschoolers' use of primitive reasoning

19 A general representation in memory of a series of events

20 The system of rules that determines how our thoughts can be expressed

Flash Cards

How long does the preoperational period last?	In what three ways is preoperational thought superior to sensorimotor thought?
According to Piaget, what is the relationship between language and thought?	In Piagetian terms, what are the limitations of preoperational thought?
Give an example of centration.	How might egocentric preschoolers behave?
Why do preschoolers fail conservation problems?	Why are preschoolers' autobiographical memories so inaccurate?
What rules do preschoolers use when counting?	According to information processors, why do preschoolers develop the ability to solve conservation problems?

It is more rapid, it is not tied to the present, and several things can be thought about simultaneously.

from 2 years of age to 7 years of age

Preschoolers do not yet have mental operations, they centrate, they are egocentric, and they have trouble with transformations.

He believed they were intertwined, but that language grows out of cognitive development, not *vice versa.*

They talk to themselves, ignore others, don't hide their nonverbal displeasure, and think they are hidden if they can't see.

A child does not notice that a roll of play dough gets skinnier as it gets longer.

Preschoolers over-rely upon scripts, they do not understand causality, and they are vulnerable to suggestion.

Due to centration, they concentrate on only one dimension, and they can't envision the transformations.

Their centration goes away because their ability to attend improves.

They assign only one name to each number, they name each number only once, and they know the names have a fixed order.

What is the significance of the fact that preschoolers sometimes say "runned" instead of "ran?"

Give examples of language pragmatics.

What happens to private speech as children get older?

What are two errors Piaget made when discussing preschooler language?

Name the three types of early education discussed in your text.

Contrast day-care centers and preschools proper.

Contrast the social benefits and costs of attending preschool programs.

Which children benefit most from preschool attendance?

What makes for a "high quality" preschool?

Name several countries that provide better preschool opportunities than does the United States.

What Stands in the way of the United States developing a national policy on preschool education?

Contrast Chinese, Japanese, and American attitudes towards the function of preschool.

It involves turntaking, sticking to a topic, knowing stock phrases, and what should and should not be said.	It shows that they are mastering the rules of grammar.
He believed that private speech served little function and he thought that children failed to modify their speech according to their listener's needs.	It becomes even more private and is whispered, done voicelessly, and eventually becomes completely internal.
Day-care centers provide all-day care; they focus on social growth. Preschools last 3-5 hours/day and are more cognitive.	Day-care centers, preschools, and school day care.
Those who are at risk or from impoverished environments.	Children become more independent and self-confident; however, they also become less polite and more competitive.
France, Belgium, Sweden, Finland, Russia	The overall group size should be small, there should be a low student/teacher ratio, and the curriculum should be well-designed.
The Chinese emphasize cognitive growth, the Japanese, a group experience, and Americans, fostering independence.	The fact that we have traditionally left schooling up to the states and to local districts

When did Head Start begin?

What evidence suggests that Head Start has worked?

Why does psychologist David Elkind argue against preschool?

Why can't we be sure that watching *Sesame Street* causes cognitive gains?

It is cost-effective, its graduates are less likely to repeat a grade or to get into trouble in school, and they are more likely to graduate.

In the 1960s as part of the War on Poverty

Parents choose whether to let their children watch or not, and they may treat their children differently in other ways as well (i.e., it's not the viewing).

He believes that young American children are too stressed and pressured.

Practice Test One

1. After 5-year old Tammy watched a cartoon with her father, he asked her to describe the plot to him. All Tammy could say was, "The dog had big spots all over!"; she hadn't noticed what the dog had been doing. This is an example of
   a. egocentrism.
   c. functionality.
   b. induction.
   d. centration.

2. Which of the following is an example of a conservation problem?
   a. Asking whether there are more pink roses or roses in a bunch of flowers.
   b. Asking whether two lines — one longer than the other — contains the same number of checkers.
   c. Asking whether the person seated across from the child can see the doll.
   d. Asking a child to arrange a set of sticks from smallest to largest.

3. Piaget
   a. believed that preschoolers know less about numbers than they actually do.
   b. thought that preschoolers are less egocentric then they actually are.
   c. believed that preschoolers could solve conservation problems when they in fact cannot.
   d. thought that preschoolers understand transformations better than they actually do.

4. Scripts are used by preschoolers to help them
   a. remember.
   c. recognize others.
   b. count.
   d. learn language.

5. Juan would really like his 5-year-old son to someday take over his architecture firm. In order to help ensure that his son has the needed spatial skills, Juan should
   a. have his son join a soccer team.
   b. coach his son in mathematics.
   c. enroll his son in piano lessons.
   d. encourage his son to become an early reader.

6. According to Lev Vygotsky, working on what type of problem would most help improve a preschooler's thinking?
   a. working on a problem that they can already easily do
   b. working on a problem that they can do with difficulty
   c. working on a problem just beyond their ability to do on their own
   d. working on a problem quite a bit harder than they can do on their own

7. David is 5 1/2 years old. He will probably
   a. correctly say "one sock" and "three socks".
   b. say "thank you" if you give him a cookie.
   c. say "Give me *the* car" instead of "Give me car".
   d. do all of the above.

8. Social speech is used
   a. to help children think.
   b. to help them control their own behavior.
   c. to communicate.
   d. to remember.

9. Poverty-class parents
   a. spend more time talking to their children than middle-class parents.
   b. are less likely to say "no" or "don't" to their children than are middle-class parents.
   c. spend more time interacting with their children than do middle-class parents.
   d. give their children less psychological support than do middle-class parents.

10. Which type of program is frequently designed with lower-income children in mind?
    a. day-care centers
    b. preschools
    c. nursery schools
    d. school day care

11. Children who attend high-quality preschool care are less
    a. compliant than other children.
    b. verbal than other children.
    c. socially-skilled than other children.
    d. independent than other children.

12. Which of the following statements is true?
    a. America has the highest quality of preschool care in the world.
    b. America has very high-quality preschool care, although several other countries provide even better care.
    c. American preschool care is about on a par with most other countries.
    d. America provides less high-quality preschool experiences than do many other countries.

13. What is the one way that Head Start programs do not succeed?
    a. Its graduates are more likely to drop out of school.
    b. Its graduates are more likely to get into trouble in school.
    c. Its graduates do not have higher IQs than students who didn't attend.
    d. It is not cost-effective.

14. Jaina is 5 years old and lives in central Chicago. How many hours of television does she likely watch per week?
    a. less than 7
    b. between 7 and 12
    c. between 14 and 20
    d. between 20 and 30

15. Which of the following is *not* an outcome of watching *Sesame Street* as a young child?
    a. reading more than one's peers
    b. being bored in school
    c. knowing one's alphabet better than one's peers
    d. having a larger vocabulary than one's peers

16. Preschool education should be
    a. done at home.
    b. done one-on-one.
    c. individualized.
    d. all of the above

Test Solutions

Self-Quiz Solution

1. d (page 253)
2. b (page 256)
3. a (page 257)
4. a (page 259)
5. c (page 260)
6. c (page 261)
7. d (page 263)
8. c (page 265)

9. d (page 266)
10. d. (page 268)
11. a (page 270)
12. d (page 271)
13. c (page 273)
14. d (page 274)
15. b (page 276)
16. c (page 277)

Crossword Puzzle Solution

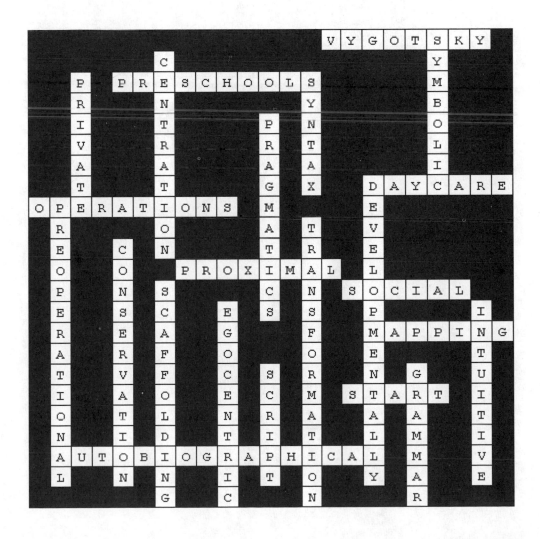

CHAPTER 9

Social and Personality Development in the Preschool Years

INTERESTING AND IMPORTANT THINGS YOU'LL KNOW AFTER READING THIS CHAPTER...

1. When do children develop gender stereotypes? See page 286.

2. At what age do children begin to have true friends? See page 292.

3. What kinds of parents have the most successful children? See page 296.

4. At what age do children begin to feel empathy for others? See page 303.

5. Why are some children so aggressive? See page 305.

Learning Objectives

When you have mastered the material in this chapter, you should be able to ...

1. Characterize preschoolers' self-concepts and describe the influences on those self-concepts. (page 284)

2. Describe the two psychosocial stages of personality development that occur during the preschool years. (page 285)

3. Explain what is meant by "racial dissonance" and describe preschoolers' understanding of the social import of race and ethnicity. (page 285)

4. Discuss the emergence of gender identity and gender stereotypes during the preschool years. (page 286)

5. Contrast the biological psychoanalytic, social learning, and cognitive approaches to gender role development. (page 287)

6. Relate how and when true friendships emerge. (page 292)

7. Characterize popular children and explain how children can be helped to become more popular. (page 293)

8. Contrast the six types of play engaged in by preschoolers. (page 294)

9. Compare the three major parenting styles, explaining which is best and why. (page 296)

10. Describe differences in American and Chinese beliefs about appropriate parenting practices. (page 298)

11. Give several suggestions as to how to best discipline children. (page 299)

12. Describe and critique Piaget's scheme of moral development. (page 301)

13. Explain the social learning approach to moral development. (page 302)

14. Discuss the development of empathy and understand its relation to moral behavior. (page 303)

15. Contrast normal and abnormal aggression in preschoolers. (page 304)

16. Discuss the strengths and weakness of the sociobiological, social learning, and cognitive approaches to aggression. (page 305)

17. Critique the data which relates violence on television to aggression in children. (page 307)

18. Provide some practical tips on how parents can reduce their preschoolers' aggressive behavior. (page 310)

Guided Review

Forming a Sense of Self

People's _____ refer to the set of beliefs that they have about themselves. Preschoolers typically _____ their own abilities and are _____ about their futures. Besides parents, _____ also influences self-image. Asian societies tend to promote a _____ orientation and promote a belief in _____. In contrast, Western cultures are more _____, which emphasizes individuals' _____ and encourages _____.

self-concepts (284)
overestimate (284)
optimistic (284)
culture (284)
collectivistic (284)
interdependence (284); individualistic (284); uniqueness (284); competition (284)

Erikson's _____ development continues during the preschool years. Early on, 1 1/2- to ____ year olds are still in the _____ vs. shame and doubt stage, a holdover from infancy. Parents should ideally encourage _____ during this stage. Later, from _____, children are in the _____ vs. guilt stage. During this stage children must learn to balance their desire for _____ with the _____ consequences that sometimes result from their actions.

psychosocial (285)
3- (285)
autonomy (285)
exploration (285)
3 until 6 (285); initiative (285)

independence (285); negative (285)

By the time children reach _____ years of age, they begin to understand the social significance of _____. Some minority preschoolers exhibit racial _____ and prefer majority values or persons more than members of their own group. However, these preferences, which are _____, do not seem to lower _____ in minority children.

3 or 4 (285)
race (285)
dissonance (285)

common (285)
self-esteem (285)

A child's sense of gender is _____ established by the time he or she reaches preschool. Children tend to sex-segregate when they _____, with girls exhibiting this preferences a little _____ than boys. Gender even outweighs _____ when it comes to choosing play partners. Children's ideas about self-appropriate behavior are more _____ than those of adults. This inflexibility peaks at about ____. Preschoolers' gender stereotypes are similar in _____ to those of adults: boys are expected to be _____ and _____, whereas girls are supposed to be _____ and _____.

well (286)

play (286)
earlier (286); ethnicity (286)

rigid (286)
5 (286)
content (286)
independent (287)
competitive (287); warm (287); submissive (287)

physical (287)

androgens (287)
masculine (287)

feminine (287)
callosum (287)

inevitable (288); experience (288)
Freud (288)
phallic (288)

castration (288); penis (288)
identify (288); same-sex (288)
do not (288)

observing (288)
television (288); teach (289)

identities (289); schemas (289)

rigid (289); appearance (290)

constancy (290); fixed (290)
does not (290)

androgynous (290)
both (290)

3 (293)

share activities (293)
trust and support (293)

Biological perspectives on gender differences claim that _____ differences cause gender differences. Evidence in support of these theories includes the fact that women who took _____ while pregnant have daughters who act more _____ than those who did not. Similarly, boys exposed to high levels of female hormones *in utero* behave in a _____ manner. Remember, too, that certain brain structures, such as the corpus _____ are different sizes in males and females. However, no one knows whether these differences are _____ or the result of _____.

According to psychoanalysts such as _____, preschoolers are in the _____ stage of personality development. These theorists propose that during this time, boys develop _____ anxiety while girls develop _____ envy. The end result is that both _____ with their _____ parents. Most developmental psychologists _____ support this view.

Social learning theorists believe that children learn gender roles by _____ others, including others that they see on _____. Sometimes parents and teachers directly _____ children to behave in gender-stereotypical ways.

According to cognitive theorists, children develop gender _____ by using gender _____, or rules about what is and is not appropriate. These beliefs are usually very _____ and are often based upon physical _____. By the time they are 4 or 5, children have developed gender _____, and understand that gender is _____. Gender constancy _____ appear to cause stereotypical behavior. Sandra Bem encourages parents to teach their children to become _____; that is, to have the characteristics of _____ genders.

Preschoolers' Social Lives

Children develop real friendships at about _____ years of age. These children view friends as people with whom to _____; as they get older, they focus more on _____.

Popular preschoolers tend to be physically _____ (although this is not as important as _____). Popular children are _____, they smile _____, and are sensitive to others' _____ behavior. Fortunately, less popular children can be _____ social skills. _____, nurturant parents tend to have popular children.

attractive (293)
social skills (293)
cooperative (293); more (293)
nonverbal (293)
taught (294); Warm (294)

Preschoolers engage in six types of play. Perhaps the simplest form (characteristic of _____ -year olds) is repetitious, _____ play. By the time children are _____, they engage in _____ play and work at building things. This type of play helps improve their _____ skills. Play becomes more _____ as children mature. At first, they typically engage in passive _____ play, or they engage in _____ play as they work side-by-side without interacting. In _____ play, children use the same materials but do _____ things. Finally, in _____ play, children begin taking _____ and playing _____. In addition, play becomes increasingly _____ as children get older.

3 (294)
functional (294); 4 (294)
constructive (294)
cognitive and physical (294)
social (294)
onlooker (295); parallel (295)

associative (295)
different (296); cooperative (295); turns (295); games (295)
unrealistic (295)

Parents have different ways of disciplining their children. _____ parents tend to be _____ and _____. _____ parents, on the other hand, are lax and require _____ of their children. (Permissive-_____ parents typically ignore their children; permissive-_____ parents are more involved with their children but place no _____ upon their behavior.) _____ parents are relatively _____, but they try to _____ with their children and allow the children to _____.

Authoritarian (296); strict (296); rigid (296); Permissive (296); little (296); indifferent (296)
indulgent (297)
restrictions (297)
Authoritative (297); strict (297)
reason (297)
disagree (297)

Children of authoritarian parents are often _____ and _____ around peers. Girls may be _____ and boys _____. Children of permissive parents have few _____ and little _____. Children of authoritative parents are _____, cooperative, and _____.

withdrawn (297)
uneasy (297); dependent (297)
hostile (297); social skills (298)
self-control (298)
independent (298); likable (298)

The above descriptions apply primarily to _____ families. Chinese parents, for example, are generally quite _____ (as were American parents until _____).

Western (298)
authoritarian (298)
World War II (299)

All children need to be disciplined. For American parents, the _____ style, with its _____, appears to be best. It is never necessary to _____ children: doing so makes them _____ and doesn't work well. Parents should adjust their strategies according to the child's _____. Many potentially difficult situations can be successfully defused with _____.

authoritative (299); explanations (299); spank (299)
aggressive (299)
temperament (299)

humor (300)

heteronomous (301)
3-7 (301)
rigid adherence (301)
shared (301)
intention (302)
imminent (302)
immediately (302)
incipient (301)
one correct (301)

10 (301); autonomous (301)
changed (302)
agree (302); underestimated (302)

decisions (302)
prosocial (302)
reinforcement (302); modeling (303); abstract modeling (303)
rules (303);
support (303)

Empathy (303)
sympathy (303)
shame (303)
guilt (303)
superego (303); Oedipal (303)

intentional (304)
cannot (304)
goal (305)
abnormal (305)
decreases (305)
stable (305)

instinct (305); little (305)

rewarded (306)
observe (306)

Piaget termed the initial stage of moral development _____ morality; he believed it lasted from about _____ years of age. This stage is characterized by a _____ to rules. These rules are not necessarily _____, however. Children in this stage do not take _____ into account when making moral judgments, and they believe in _____ justice. That is, they think that misbehavior will be _____ punished. Play becomes more truly social when children develop _____ cooperation, although they continue to believe that there is only _____ way to play. The most advanced form of morality develops at _____; Piaget termed it the _____ cooperation stage. Children now understand that rules can be _____ if the participants _____ to do so. Piaget generally _____ children's moral development.

Whereas Piaget emphasized moral _____, the social learning theorists are more interested in _____ behavior. They acquire this behavior through _____ and _____. Through _____, children not only learn what to do in specific circumstances, but also learn general _____. The data for the most part _____ this perspective.

_____ — knowing what another is feeling — encourages moral behavior. Other emotions, such as _____ and _____, also contribute to it. Freud emphasized the role of _____ in moral development: he believed that the _____, which develops as a result of the _____ complex, motivates children to behave morally.

Aggression is the _____ harm of another. Infants, therefore, _____ behave aggressively. Much preschooler aggression is performed in an attempt to attain some _____. Extreme or sustained aggression is _____. Generally, aggression _____ during the course of the preschool years. Relative aggression level is a _____ trait.

Freud and Lorenz shared the view that aggression is a human _____. This view has received _____ experimental support. Social learning theorists contend that children become aggressive when they are _____ for aggressive behavior or when they _____ it around them.

Most children are exposed to violence on _____. The bulk of the research examining its effects is _____, but the data strongly suggests that watching violent programs _____ aggression. Similarly, watching nonaggressive models _____ aggression.

television (307)
correlational (307)

increases (308)
reduces (308)

The cognitive approach to aggression says that some children are aggressive because they _____ others' nonverbal signals as _____. The main strength of this approach is that it provides clues to one means of _____ aggression.

misinterpret (309)
hostile (309)
reducing (309)

How can we help children grow up to be nonaggressive? We can provide them with _____ models. We can have them work with peers towards a _____ goal. Parents _____ ignore their children's aggression and assume they will outgrow it, and they should teach their children _____ and _____ ways of dealing with their anger.

nonaggressive (310)
common (310)
should not (311)

self-control (311); alternative (311)

Crossword Puzzle

Social and Personality Development In the Preschool Years

Across

1 _____ parents are firm, but they reason with their children.

4 _____ development involves changes in a person's sense of right and wrong.

8 Scientists who study the biological roots of social behavior

10 Race _____ occurs when minority children prefer the attributes of the majority

11 The _____ perspective was developed by Erikson.

12 These parents exercise little control over their children.

14 _____ justice

15 Gender _____: the understanding that individuals are permanently male or female

18 Individuals who possess characteristics both stereotypically masculine and stereotypically feminine

19 An emotional response that corresponds to the emotions of another person

20 _____ vs. guilt

21 Gender _____: the sense one has of oneself as male or female

22 _____ play occurs when children watch each other play.

Down

2 _____ orientation: philosophy that emphasizes personal identity and uniqueness

3 _____ play: e.g., two children share crayons, but each work on their own drawings

5 _____ parents are controlling and punitive.

6 _____ orientation: a philosophy that promotes the notion of interdependence

7 _____ play occurs when children build something.

9 A process in which children attempt to be similar to their same-sex parent

11 _____ behavior helps others.

13 _____ morality: rules are seen as inviolable and unchanging

15 _____ play: e.g., playing house or cards or basketball

16 Gender _____: a cognitive framework that organizes information relevant to gender

17 _____ play involves simple, repetitive actions.

18 The intentional injury of another

Flash Cards

In what way are preschoolers' self-concepts inaccurate?	Contrast collectivist and individualistic orientations.
How can parents help their children through the initiative vs. guilt psychosocial crisis?	Which two Eriksonian crises occur during the preschool period?
What is the relationship between race dissonance and self-esteem?	Give a piece of evidence which supports the biological perspective of gender differences.
Why can't we conclude that brain differences in men and women cause gender differences in behavior?	Which Freudian psychosexual stage occurs during the preschool years?
According to Freud, what drives identification in boys? In girls?	Contrast the terms gender schema, gender identity, and gender constancy.

Collectivist societies emphasize coorperation and interdependence; individualistic societies emphasize independence and uniqueness.	They overestimate their own abilities and are overly optimistic about their chances for future success.
The latter half of the autonomy vs. shame and doubt crisis and the initiative vs. guilt crisis	Parents can give children opportunities to act self-reliantly while being supportive and providing guidance as needed.
Girls exposed to androgens prenatally behave in a masculine fashion; vice versa for boys exposed to high levels of female hormones.	There is none: children with race dissonance may have high self-esteem.
The phallic stage	It's a chicken and egg problem: we don't know which came first and caused the other.
Gender schema is a cognitive framework; gender identity is the sense of oneself as male or female; gender constancy is the knowledge that one's sex doesn't change.	In boys it is castration anxiety; in girls it is penis envy.

List some traits characteristic of unpopular children.	Give an example of functional play.
Give an example of constructive play.	Contrast parallel and associative play.
Why does play become increasingly unrealistic as children mature?	Contrast authoritarian and authoritative parents.
In what ways are children raised by authoritarian and permissive parents similar?	Describe children raised by authoritative parents.
Why is spanking ill-advised?	Describe Lawrence Steinberg's controversial stance on discipline.
What is the main problem with Piaget's conception of moral development?	According to social learning theorists, what two mechanisms account for moral development?

Skipping, rolling a toy car back and forth, banging two sticks together	They are physically unattractive, aggressive, disruptive, and uncooperative.
In parallel play, children use the same materials but do not interact; in associative play, they share or borrow toys but do not work together.	Building a house out of blocks, making a puzzle, making a stick-figure out of clay
Authoritarian parents are controlling and punitive. Authoritative parents, while strict, explain their actions to their children and reason with them.	Because new-found mental abilities let children stretch their imaginations further (e.g., you don't need a toy train, because a box can be a train)
They are independent, friendly, self-assured, cooperative, successful, and likable.	They lack social skills and are dependent.
Steinberg believes that economically disadvantaged children benefit from authoritarian parenting.	Because it doesn't work very well and it leads to aggressive behavior
Reinforcement and modeling	Piaget underestimated the rate at which moral development occurs.

What is the difference between modeling and abstract modeling?

How is empathy related to moral behavior?

Name several emotions that can motivate moral behavior.

Why can't infants behave aggressively?

What is meant by the statement: "Aggression is a relatively stable trait."

What is Freud's explanation for human aggression?

Describe Bandura's classic study of the power of observational learning.

Why shouldn't parents ignore their preschoolers' aggressive behavior?

Children are more likely to behave morally if they can understand when they've hurt others.	Modeling means to copy just what you see; abstract modeling involves copying the underlying rules of behavior.
Because they are too immature to behave intentionally.	Empathy, sympathy, admiration, anger, guilt, shame
He believed that we all have a self-destructive "death wish," and that aggression is this hostility turned outwards.	It means that the most aggressive preschoolers will most likely grow up to be aggressive adults.
Because aggression is often self-rewarding (e.g., you get the candy by knocking down the smaller child) it won't go away on its own.	Bandura showed children a nonviolent control film or a film of an adult abusing a Bobo doll; those who saw the aggressive models were more aggressive.

Practice Test One

1. Chi-chaun is 5 years old and newly immigrated with her family from Taiwan. She most likely believes
   a. that she is very different from other children and very special.
   b. that it is very important to stand out and be the best in her class.
   c. that she could easily outrun her classmates.
   d. that she is a failure.

2. Levon is 5 1/2 years old. Which Eriksonian crisis is he most likely experiencing?
   a. basic trust vs. mistrust
   b. initiative vs. quilt
   c. industry vs. inferiority
   d. autonomy vs. shame and doubt

3. Ethnic identity
   a. develops during the preschool years.
   b. leads to low self-esteem.
   c. prevents the occurrence of race dissonance.
   d. is most likely to develop when children are raised bilingually.

4. Preschooler cross-sex play
   a. is common in most societies, but not in America.
   b. is common in America but not in many other countries.
   c. in not common in America nor is it common in most other countries.
   d. is common in all societies, including America.

5. Which of the following terms refers to the cognitive framework that children develop to help them understand gender?
   a. gender schema
   b. gender identity
   c. gender constancy
   d. gender role

6. Young preschoolers see friends as people you
   a. can do things with.
   b. can trust.
   c. can talk to.
   d. can count on to help you.

7. Which of the following would help an unpopular child become more popular?
   a. teaching her to pay attention to others' nonverbal signals
   b. teaching him to take turns
   c. teaching her to be more positive
   d. all of the above

8. The most developmentally advanced form of play is
   a. associative play.
   b. parallel play.
   c. constructive play.
   d. cooperative play.

9. Which of the following is the best parenting strategy to adopt?
   a. authoritative
   b. authoritarian
   c. permissive-indulgent
   d. permissive-indifferent

10. The Chinese believe that the best parents
    a. are permissive and indulgent with their children.
    b. spend a good deal of time answering children's questions.
    c. are strict and firm and in control.
    d. encourage their children to be creative and independent.

11. The best forms of discipline
    a. include spanking.
    b. include explanations.
    c. require obedience for obedience's sake.
    d. encourage children to set their own standards of behavior.

12. According to Piaget, which develops last?
    a. a belief in imminent justice
    b. heteronomous morality
    c. incipient cooperation
    d. autonomous cooperation

13. Which theorists are most interested in the development of prosocial behavior?
    a. sociobiologists
    b. psychoanalysts
    c. social learning theorists
    d. cognitive theorists

14. Which is the earliest evidence of empathy?
    a. one-year olds crying when they hear another baby cry
    b. two-year olds offering gifts to others
    c. three-year olds patting the back of a crying child
    d. four-year olds getting angry when another child is treated unfairly

15. What is the most common sort of aggression in preschoolers?
    a. hitting another after losing one's temper because one has lost a game
    b. shoving another child so that one can get in the front of the line
    c. biting another child simply for the pleasure of seeing that other child cry
    d. hitting one's father because one is in a bad mood

16. Of the different approaches to moral development described in your text, it is clear that Bob Feldman (the author) favors the
    a. sociobiological perspective.
    b. psychoanalytic perspective.
    c. social learning perspective.
    d. cognitive development perspective.

17. Which of the following statements is true?
    a. There is a good deal of clear, compelling experimental data proving that watching violent television causes aggression.
    b. There is a good deal of correlational data which proves that watching violent television causes aggression.
    c. There is a good deal of correlational data which suggests that watching violent television causes aggression.
    d. There is actually very little data linking violent television and aggressive behavior.

18. Which is the most useful thing to say if you catch your 5-year-old daughter stealing her brother's pennies?
    a. Nice girls don't steal!
    b. You will be punished if you do anything like that again!
    c. You should know better!
    d. Your brother would be so sad to lose his hard-earned pennies!

Test Solutions

Self-Quiz Solution

1. c (page 284)
2. b (page 285)
3. d (page 285)
4. c (page 286)
5. d (page 289)
6. a (page 293)
7. d (page 293)
8. d (page 295)
9. a (page 297)

10. c. (page 298)
11. b (page 299)
12. d (page 301)
13. c (page 302)
14. a (page 303)
15. b (page 304)
16. c (page 305)
17. c (page 307)
18. d (page 310)

Crossword Puzzle Solution

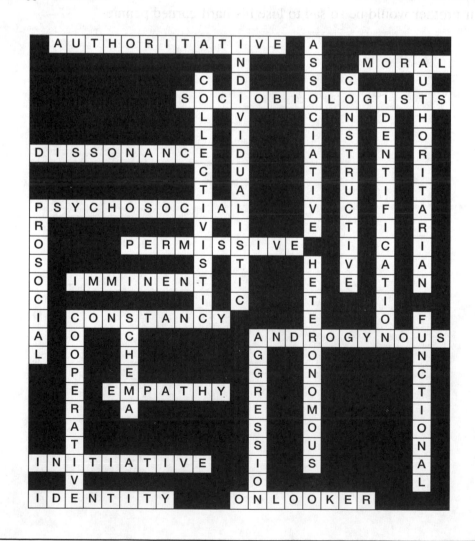

CHAPTER 10

Physical Development in Middle Childhood

INTERESTING AND IMPORTANT THINGS YOU'LL KNOW AFTER READING THIS CHAPTER...

THE GROWING BODY

MOTOR DEVELOPMENT AND SAFETY

CHILDREN WITH SPECIAL NEEDS

Learning Objectives

When you have mastered the material in this chapter, you should be able to ...

1. Characterize the pace and extent of physical growth during middle childhood. (page 320)

2. Discuss the use of artificial growth hormones to increase the height of short children. (page 321)

3. Describe the link between under-nutrition and social and cognitive development. (page 322)

4. Enumerate the causes of childhood obesity. (page 323)

5. Discuss the symptoms and incidence of childhood asthma. (page 325)

6. Identify and describe two psychological disorders that occur in middle childhood. (page 325)

7. Outline steps that parents can take to successfully encourage their children to exercise. (page 326)

8. Describe gross motor advances in middle childhood and explain the causes of gender differences in motor abilities. (page 328)

9. Discuss the development of fine motor skills during middle childhood and know why these advances occur. (page 329)

10. Understand the relationship between physical prowess and popularity during middle school. (page 330)

11. Explain the major causes of children's accidents and know how to help prevent them. (page 330)

12. Provide guidelines for children's safe use of the Internet. (page 331)

13. Understand the problems posed by visual, auditory and speech impairments. (page 334)

14. Define the term "learning disability" and be able to describe the most common type. (page 335)

15. Enumerate the symptoms of ADHD and know the problems with using drugs to treat it. (page 336)

16. Describe the practice of mainstreaming and discuss its advantages. (page 337)

Guided Review

The Growing Body

Growth during middle childhood is _____ and _____. Throughout elementary school, children put on _____ inches per year and gain about _____ pounds per year. At the end of this stage, girls are slightly _____ than boys. Most height differences in American children are caused by _____; however, in many countries, some children's heights are influenced by _____.

slow (320); steady (320)
2-3(320)
5-7 (320)
taller (320)
genetics (321)

nutrition (321)

_____ is an artificial growth _____ that helps short children grow taller. Approximately _____ American children are taking such drugs. Although they do add inches, these drugs also have _____. The American Academy of Pediatrics recommends that only those children with _____ levels of growth hormone be given these injections.

Protropin (321); hormone (321)
20,000 (322)

side-effects (322)

subnormal (322)

Children who are malnourished are not only shorter than other children, but they exhibit social and personality effects as well. Malnourished children are _____ involved with peers, are more _____, are less _____, are less willing to _____, and are less _____ than properly nourished children.

less (322)
anxious (322); alert (322)
explore (322); self-confident (322)

In addition, these children are less curious and _____ than well-fed children.

responsive (323)

Paradoxically, although many children are concerned with being slim, childhood obesity is on the _____. Obesity is caused by a combination of _____, parental _____ of eating, lack of _____, and excessive _____. Television contributes to obesity because it is a _____ activity and because it encourages _____.

rise (323)
genetics (323); over-control (323); exercise; (323); TV (324); sedentary (323)
snacking (324)

Most children are quite _____ during middle childhood, although most will have at least _____ serious illness during this stage of life and about _____ have a chronic medical condition.

healthy (324)
one (324)
11% (324)

Asthma (325)
wheezing (325)
infection (325); allergic (325)
exercise (325); pollution (325)

depression (325)

adults' (325)
clingy (325); fears (325)
delinquency (325); 8-9% (326)
anxiety (326)
specific (326)
generalized (326)

fun (326); partner (326)
organized (327); slowly (326);
punishment (327)

bicycle (328)
rope (328); outperform (329)

sports (329)
encouragement (329)

cursive (329); typing (329); 11
or 12 (329)
myelin (330); neural (330)

boys (330)

early (330)

playing (330)
winning (330)

_____ rates are increasing rapidly. This condition is characterized by _____ and shortness of breath. Attacks can be triggered by _____, _____ reactions, stress, and _____. Increased air _____ may be at least partially responsible for its increase.

Childhood _____ is a psychological disorder that was frequently overlooked, in good part because children's symptoms do not match _____ symptoms. Depressed children become _____, develop _____, sulk, and provoke acts of _____. In addition, about _____ of children suffer from _____ disorders. Some of these children have _____ fears (such as insects) while others have bouts of _____ anxiety.

Parents can encourage their children to exercise by making it _____. Finding a _____ helps, as does joining an _____ group. Children should start _____. Never use exercise as _____.

Motor Development and Safety

Gross motor development really takes off during middle childhood. Most children master _____ riding, swimming, and jumping _____ at this time. Boys generally _____ girls, but much of this difference seems to be attributable to the fact that boys participate more in _____ and receive more _____.

Fine motor skills also improve. Children master writing in _____ and _____ on a keyboard. By _____, fine motor abilities are almost at adult levels. This is primarily due to increased _____ levels, which speed _____ transmission.

Children, especially _____, tend to be more popular if good at sports. The contributions of athletic success, however, is confounded with those of _____ physical maturation, since these usually co-occur. In order to minimize the stigma of being a mediocre athlete, children should be taught that the pleasure of sports comes in the _____, not the _____.

_____children are more likely to be physically injured than younger children, and _____ are more likely to have accidents than girls. _____ represent the greatest threat to children. _____, drowning, _____ injuries and bicycle accidents are also all too common. Children should always wear _____ when in a car, and _____ when riding bikes. Younger children should not mix with older children when playing _____ sports.

Older (330)
boys (330)
Automobiles (330)
Fires (33); gun-related (330)

seat belts (331); helmets (331)

contact (331)

Children who use the Internet are at risk for exposure to _____ and may make contact with unsavory persons in chat rooms. Children should be taught never to provide _____ information when on-line, and parents should closely _____ their Web experiences.

pornography (331)

personal (332)
monitor (332)

Children with Special Needs

Visual impairments include _____ and _____ sight-edness. Blind individuals have visual acuities of less than _____; partially-sighted individuals have visual acuities of less than _____. Even when a child does not meet these legal criteria, he or she might have problems in _____, which requires _____ vision. About _____ children need special education due to visual difficulties. Warning signs include redness, _____, facial contortions and _____. People with poor vision tend to hold books _____ when they read.

blindness (334); partial (334)

20/200 (334)
20/70 (334)

school (334); close-up (334)
1/1000 (334)
blinking (335)
headaches (335)
close (335)

Auditory impairments, which affect ____ of children, can affect _____ as well as school performance. Some children have difficulty hearing only certain _____. Since hearing loss affects _____ development, children who lose their hearing before the age of ____ are more affected than those whose loss comes later.

1-2% (335)
social relations (335)
frequencies (335)
language (335)
3 (335)

Hearing loss is frequently accompanied by _____ impairment. _____ of children have this problem, which is diagnosed whenever a child's speech _____ to itself, interferes with _____, or _____ the speaker. The most common speech disorder is _____.

speech (335)
3-5% (335)
calls attention (335)
communication (335); distresses (335) stuttering (335)

learning disabilities (336)
actual (336)
potential (336)
listening (335); speaking (335);
writing (335); mathematics (335)
Dyslexia (336); letters (336)
spelling (336)
genetic (336); environmental
(336)
attention (336)
inattentive (336); impulsive
(336); frustrated (336)
self-control (336); distracted
(336); Ritalin (336); stimulant
(336); attention-span (336); com-
pliance (336)

PL94-142 (337)

least restrictive (336)

mainstreaming (338); as much
(338)
labeling (338); negative (338)

disabled (338); typical (338)
full inclusion (338)
all (338)
entire (338)

The umbrella term _____ is used for children who exhibit a discrepancy between their _____ learning and their _____ for learning. Children may have difficulty _____, _____, reading, _____, reasoning, or in doing _____. _____, a specific form of reading disability, occurs when children reverse _____ and have trouble _____ correctly. Learning disabilities are caused by both _____ and _____ factors.

ADHD, or _____-deficit hyperactivity disorder, causes a child to be _____, to be _____, to be easily _____, and to move constantly and fidget. These children have limited _____ and are readily _____. Many of these children are given _____, a type of _____. Although in the short run stimulants can increase _____ and _____, the long-term effects are not as positive.

In 1975, Congress passed _____, the Education for All Handicapped Children Act. The main thrust of this law was that disabled children should be taught in the _____ environment, a practice that has come to be known as _____. This means that disabled children spend _____ of the day integrated into regular classrooms as possible. This practice helps avoid _____, with its _____ consequences. Mainstreaming has been found to benefit both _____ and _____ children. More extreme and more controversial is the practice of _____; if this practice were to take hold, _____ students would spend their _____ day in regular classrooms.

Crossword Puzzle

Physical Development In Middle Childhood

Across

4   _____ blindness: acuity of less than 20/200

7   Learning _____ make it difficult for some children to understand spoken or written language or mathematics.

8   Visual _____ include blindness and partial sightedness.

9   A stimulant used to treat children with ADHD

10 The "least _____ environment"

11 _____ impairments involve either a partial or total hearing loss.

14 Attention-deficit _____ disorder

15 The most common speech impairment

16 Full _____ is the mainstreaming of all students into regular classrooms.

Down

1   The sound made when a person has an asthmatic attack

2   _____ disorders cause children to be feel intensely nervous and uncomfortable.

3   Childhood _____ was unrecognized until fairly recently.

5   A medical condition which causes individuals to have trouble breathing

6   An educational approach in which disabled children are placed into regular classrooms as much as possible.

12 The condition of being more than 20% above normal body weight

13 _____ sightedness: acuity of less than 20/70 after correction

Flash Cards

At what age are girls taller than boys, and why then?	What factors in addition to genetics could help account for ethnic height differences?
Why might some parents want their short children to receive artificial growth hormone?	What are the risks of giving children artificial growth hormone?
According to one study cited in your text, what percentage of American children can pass the fitness standards set by the US government?	What is the best strategy to help obese children lose weight?
Why are there so few life-threatening illnesses associated with middle-schoolers?	Why has the rate of asthma been increasing?
Why are poor children more likely to be asthmatic than middle-class children?	Name several factors that can trigger an asthma attack.

Dietary customs and socioeconomic differences could also contribute to height differences.

At about 11, because girls have already begun their adolescent growth spurts and boys haven't

It may make them more susceptible to infections and it may retard later growth by speeding up puberty.

To prevent the social stigma and teasing that can come with being abnormally small

Rather than directly working on weight loss, the goal should be weight stabilization: over time, the child's growth will normalize his or her weight.

One-third

Factors include: increased air pollution, more correct diagnoses, and less drafty (and hence more dusty) housing.

American children are immunized against the worst childhood diseases and so do not contract them.

Stress, exercise, allergic responses, and infections

They receive less and poorer medical care and they are exposed to more pollutants.

How can childhood depression
be distinguished from
normal childhood sadness?

Should elementary-aged boys and
girls play on sports teams
together?

What evidence argues against the
fact that boys' substantial
superiority in athletics is genetic?

How does myelin help speed
neural impulses?

How can parents help teach
children to avoid over-emphasizing
the importance of physical prowess?

Why does the accident rate
increase during middle childhood?

Why are boys more likely to have
accidents than girls?

What are the most frequent types
of accidents in children?

Why aren't the legal definitions of
blindness and partial-sightedness
useful in the classrooms?

List some of the symptoms of
visual impairments.

Why do children who lose their
hearing before age three have a
harder time than children who
lose their hearing later?

Which are easier for deaf children
to master and why: concrete
concepts or abstract concepts?

According to the American Academy of Pediatrics, yes. Once they reach puberty, though, the sexes should be separated.	By its duration and intensity
By acting as insulation	The fact that girls who participate in team sports perform at close to male levels
Children become more mobile and independent during these years.	By not giving them messages that the goal of sports is winning
Car accidents, burns from fires, drowning, and gunshots	Boys are more physically active than girls and so the risk of injury is greater.
Red, burning eyes; blinking; squinting; messy handwriting; headaches; dizziness	Those definitions are most concerned with long-distance vision, whereas most school tasks require close-up vision.
Concrete concepts are easier, because they can be demonstrated visually.	Prior to age three, children have a limited understanding of language and have not yet learned to make all speech sounds.

How should parents try to help
a child who stutters?

Why do learning disabilities differ
from mental retardation?

Name the six abilities that may be
affected by learning disabilities.

What separates a child with
ADHD from a normally-active
child?

Why was P194-142 passed into law?

What are some of the drawbacks
of labeling children?

Contrast mainstreaming with
full inclusion.

Mentally retarded individuals have low learning potential; learning-disabled individuals have a high potential for learning, but something is impeding it.

Don't draw attention to the stuttering. Let children finish their own sentences. Get them into speech therapy.

Not finishing tasks; frequently interrupting others; starting a task without reading instructions; lack of organization

Reading, writing, listening, speaking, reasoning, mathematics

It's not precise; it sets up negative expectations; it lowers self-esteem; it sets up self-fulfilling prophesies; it causes rejection

The data showed that segregated classrooms were not working, and, philosophically, integration was believed to be best.

In mainstreaming, disabled children spend part of their day in special ed classrooms; in full inclusions, all students would be full-time in regular classes.

1. Physical growth during middle childhood can best be characterized as being
    a. accelerating and sporadic.
    b. waxing and waning.
    c. rapid and inconsistent.
    d. slow and steady.

2. Which of the following is a concern for children who use artificial growth hormones to increase their height?
    a. They may have elevated cancer rates.
    b. They may reach puberty sooner than they would have.
    c. They may become more susceptible to infection.
    d. They may not end up any taller as adults than they would have without the drug.

3. Which of the following can result from malnutrition during middle childhood?
    a. Malnourished children do not tolerate frustration as well as well-nourished children.
    b. Malnourished children are less alert than well-nourished children.
    c. Malnourished children do not perform as well on tests of verbal abilities than well-nourished children.
    d. All of the above may result from malnutrition.

4. Which of the following cannot be used to explain the recent increase in the number of obese American children?
    a. genetics
    b. lack of exercise
    c. excessive television viewing
    d. over-control of children's eating by parents

5. Which of the following does not sometimes cause asthma attacks?
    a. pollutants
    b. stress
    c. allergens
    d. malnutrition

6. Which of the following is characteristic of childhood depression but not adult depression?
    a. sadness
    b. hopelessness
    c. excessive fears
    d. a negative outlook

7. Terry's parents are concerned that she does not get enough exercise. Which might they best do to encourage her?
    a. Require Terry to exercise instead of punishing her in their usual way.
    b. Exercise with her.
    c. Buy her the best professional-grade equipment.
    d. All of the above

8. Gender differences in gross motor performance
   a. decrease during middle childhood.
   b. are genetic.
   c. are minimized if children are equally encouraged.
   d. are non-existent during middle childhood.

9. By what age do children's fine motor skills reach near-adult levels?
   a. 5-6 years
   b. 7-8 years
   c. 9-10 years
   d. 11-12 years

10. The popularity of athletic boys
    a. increases throughout middle childhood.
    b. remains stable and high during middle childhood.
    c. remains stable and low during middle childhood.
    d. decreases throughout middle childhood.

11. The single greatest cause of serious accidents in children is
    a. fire.
    b. guns.
    c. automobiles.
    d. water/drowning.

12. The book "Web of Deception" deals with
    a. advertising on the Internet.
    b. pornography on the Internet.
    c. the dangers of chat rooms on the Internet.
    d. the misuse of the Internet by children.

13. Which is the least common disorder experienced by children?
    a. visual impairments
    b. attention-deficit hyperactivity disorder
    c. speech impairment
    d. auditory impairments

14. Christina has been diagnosed with a learning disability. Which of the following is least likely to be true?
    a. Christina sees letters as if they were written backwards.
    b. Christina has difficulty spelling correctly.
    c. Christina has difficulty expressing herself orally.
    d. Christina is mentally retarded.

15. Jared just can't seem to sit still. In addition, he bounces from one task to another and does poorly in school because he never reads the directions on his papers. What other symptom would you expect Jared to have?
    a. He likely has a hearing problem.
    b. He likely is dyslexic.
    c. He likely gets easily frustrated.
    d. He likely is mentally retarded.

16. Mainstreaming
    a. is synonymous with "full inclusion".
    b. has generally benefited disabled children but not typical children.
    c. has not been supported by the data.
    d. does not mean that all children spend all of their day in regular classrooms.

Test Solution

Self-Quiz Solution

1. d (page 320)
2. a (page 322)
3. d (page 322)
4. a (page 323)
5. d (page 325)
6. c (page 325)
7. b (page 326)
8. c (page 329)

9. d (page 329)
10. a (page 330)
11. c (page 330)
12. a (page 332)
13. a (page 334)
14. d (page 335)
15. c (page 336)
16. d (page 337)

Crossword Puzzle Solution

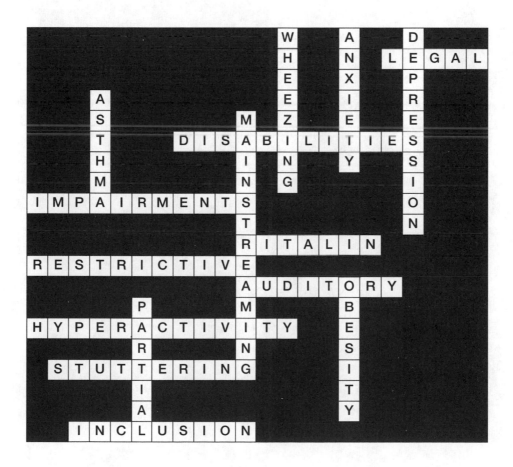

CHAPTER 11

Cognitive Development in Middle Childhood

Interesting and Important Things You'll Know After Reading This Chapter...

Learning Objectives

When you have mastered the material in this chapter, you should be able to ...

1. Characterize the cognitive advances that occur during the period of concrete operations. (page 345)

2. Critique Piaget's conception of cognition during middle childhood. (page 347)

3. Explain middle childhood cognitive advances from the information processing perspective. (page 348)

4. Describe the linguistic development common to middle childhood. (page 349)

5. Discuss the ramifications of being, and of being taught, bilingually. (page 351)

6. Describe the contention over Ebonics. (page 353)

7. Describe global school attendance rates. (page 355)

8. Explain the factors that do and do not account for school readiness. (page 355)

9. Understand how American schooling has been changing in the 1990s. (page 356)

10. Discuss the goals and models of multicultural education. (page 358)

11. Explain how student and teacher attributions can influence academic performance. (page 359)

12. Describe the first intelligence test, and understand its three legacies. (page 366)

13. Compute a person's IQ score, given their mental and chronological ages. (page 367)

14. Contrast the three most-often used intelligence tests. (page 368)

15. Describe several of the major theories of the nature of intelligence. (page 368)

16. Explain the causes of racial differences in IQ scores. (page 371)

17. Compare the functioning of people with different degrees of mental retardation. (page 374)

18. Describe the characteristics of gifted and talented children and be able to identify several approaches to helping them attain their full potential. (page 376)

19. Provide several suggestions for helping children achieve academic success. (page 377)

Guided Review

Intellectual and Language Development

Between 7 and _____ years of age, children are in Piaget's _____ operational stage of cognitive development. They can now _____, or take multiple aspects of a situation into account when solving problems. Children in this stage understand _____: that is, they can imagine untransforming an object back to its original form. Similarly, they understand _____ and know that despite changes in shape, objects remain the same. Finally they master _____, and recognize that as a piece of clay is stretched longer, it also gets more narrow. These advances let them better perceive the relationship between time and _____. Children's biggest limitation is that they cannot think about _____ concepts and _____ questions.

12 (345)
concrete (345)
decenter (345)

reversibility (345)

identity (346)

compensation (346)

speed (346)
abstract (346); hypothetical (346)

As before, Piaget tended to _____ middle-schoolers' cognitive abilities. Children are also less _____ than Piaget suggested. We also now know that not all children _____ concrete operations (although it appears that they can do so if they are _____).

underestimate (346)
consistent (346)

attain (347)
taught (347)

Information processors explain children's advances in cognition by increased _____ capacity and use of more advanced _____. In order to remember a piece of information, children must first _____ that information, then they must _____ it and finally they must _____ it from memory. In particular, _____ memory increases greatly during this life stage. _____, the understanding of how memory works, also develops. As it does, children begin to use _____ strategies. For example, at first they begin to _____ information in order to better remember it; then they begin to _____ it. Children _____ taught these strategies. One, known as the _____ strategy, is used to help children learn foreign languages.

memory (348)
strategies (348)
encode (348)
store (348); retrieve (348)
short term (349)
Metamemory (349)

control (349)
rehearse (349)
organize (349)
can be (349)
keyword (349)

Vocabulary (350)
5000 (350)
passive (350); conditional
(350)
phonemes (350)
intonation (350); social (350)
Metalinguistic (350)

explicit (350); self-control
(351)
bilingualism (352)

flexible (352); metalinguistic
(352)
easily (352)
immersion (352)

majority (353)
dominant (353)

Ebonics (353)

dialect (353)
inferior (353)

Language use improves in several ways. _____ grows by about _____ words during this period. Use of the _____ voice and _____ sentences increases. By the end of middle childhood, most children have mastered even the most difficult _____. They learn to read the nuances implied by different _____. Pragmatics, the _____ use of language, also gets better. _____ awareness develops, so that children's understanding of language's rules becomes _____. This helps them learn _____.

Psychologists are coming to realize that _____ has cognitive benefits. Bilingual individuals are more cognitively _____ and they have more _____ awareness than monolingual individuals. Elementary-aged children learn second languages _____. For example, children in language _____ programs are taught entirely in a second language. These programs are most successful when _____ children are being taught a language not spoken by the _____ culture.

In 1996, a California school board declared that _____ was a different language than Standard English. Most linguists, however, see it as a _____ of Standard English, not _____ to it but only different from it.

Schooling: The Three R's (and more) of Middle Childhood

right (355)
developing (355)
girls (355)
science (355)

does not (356)

reading (356); educational
(356)

basics (356)
accountable (356)
competency (356)
multicultural (358)

In most developed countries, education is a basic _____. In many _____ countries this is not so, and many children, especially _____, receive little or no education. And, even in developed countries, girls receive less _____ education than boys.

What makes a child ready to begin school? Age _____ appear to be a major factor. Parents' attitudes towards _____ matters more, as does their _____ background.

The trend in American education in the 1990s is a return to the _____. Another new tendency is to hold teachers _____ for their students' learning and to make students take _____ tests. As America becomes ever more diverse, increasing attention is being paid to _____ education.

Multicultural education is designed to help students from _____ groups maintain a positive ethnic identity while developing competence in the majority culture. In the past, America was viewed as a _____ pot, and a cultural _____ model was favored. That is, everyone was expected to become _____. This concept has been replaced by a _____ society model, which holds that individual groups should _____ their separate identities. A practical difference between these two approaches concerns the _____ at which children are expected to learn English and the degree to which use of their second language is _____. In addition, course material reflecting the heritage of _____ students is presented; the goal is to enhance all students' _____.

minority (358)

melting (358)
assimilation (358)
similar (358)
pluralistic (358)
retain (358)

rate (359)

encouraged (359)
all (359)
self-esteems (359)

Why do students in Asian countries learn more in school than their American counterparts? Part of the explanation may lie in the different _____ made by Americans and Asians about educational success. Asians view academic success as a result of _____ work and _____; Americans view it as more of a result of native _____. Therefore, Asian educators and students see failure as only a _____ setback. African-Americans, though, are apt to attribute school failure or success to _____ causes, such as luck or discrimination, and females are more likely than males to attribute failure to _____ and success to _____ causes.

attributions (360)

hard (360); perseverance (360)
ability (360)

temporary (360)
external (360)

low ability (361)
external (361)

In 1968, a critical study was conducted which demonstrated the power of teacher _____ effects: it showed that children in which the teachers _____ would do well actually did do well, even though they were in fact _____ from the other students. This self-fulfilling _____ is achieved because teachers are more _____ towards students they expect to do well, they give these students more positive _____ and more _____ material, and they simply spend more _____ with them. This warm climate encourages students to _____ and develop more positive _____, both of which effect performance.

expectancy (362)
believed (362)
no different (362)
prophecy (362)
positive (363)

feedback (363); difficult (363)
time (363)
work hard (363)
self-esteem (363)

Intelligence: Determining Individual Strengths

Intelligence is the capacity to understand the _____, think _____, and use resources effectively.

world (366)
rationally (366)

at the turn of (366)
Binet (366); pragmatically
(367); distinguished (367)

school (367)
mental age (367); does not
(367)
IQ (367)
quotient (367); 100 (367)
deviation (368)
2/3 (368)
115 (368)

Stanford (368)
easiest (368)
WISC-III (368)
WAIS -III (368)
verbal (369); performance
(368); Kaufman (368)
integrate (368); step-by-step
(368); good (368)
poor (368)
future success (368)

single (368)
g (368); disagree (368)
fluid (368)

crystallized (370)
seven (370)

Vygotsky (370); dynamic (371)
adult aid (371)
information processing (371)
process (371)
3 (371)
triarchic (371); Componential
(371); Experiential (371);

contextual (371)

The first intelligence test was developed _____ the century by Alfred _____. He devised his test _____, by asking students questions and keeping those that _____ between the bright and less bright. He linked intelligence and _____ success and thought they were synonymous. He converted each child's score to a _____. This _____ allow comparisons between children of different ages. To do this, one must calculate an _____ score (which stands for "intelligence _____"). The average IQ score is _____, regardless of a person's age. Today, the _____ IQ score is more often used; using this measure, _____ of everyone has an IQ score falling between 85 and _____.

One of the earliest IQ tests used in this country was modeled after Binet's and so is called the _____-Binet. The items are arranged so that the _____ questions come first. Two other IQ tests, designed by Wechsler — the _____, given to children and the _____, given to adults — give separate subscores for _____ and _____ skills. The K-ABC, or _____ Assessment Battery, measures children's ability to _____ different kinds of stimuli and to think in a _____ fashion. Scores on these tests are _____ predictors of a child's academic performance, but are _____ at predicting a person's _____.

The most frequently-used intelligence tests presume that there is a _____ underlying aspect of intelligence, called _____. Many psychologists _____ with this. One alternative conception is that two kinds of intelligence exist: _____ intelligence, which helps people deal with new problems, and _____ intelligence, which refers to learned information. Howard Gardner believes that there are _____ different types of intelligence. In keeping with his views about how learning occurs Lev _____ believed in the _____ assessment of children, so that their ability to function with _____ could be measured. Robert Sternberg has proposed an _____ theory of intelligence which looks at _____ rather than components. His theory, which breaks intelligence into _____ parts, is called the _____ theory. _____ intelligence reflects how well people can process information. _____ intelligence is insightful and allows for creativity. Finally, _____ intelligence is practical, everyday intelligence.

Many studies have shown _____ differences in average IQ score; in particular, on average African Americans score about _____ points lower than Caucasians. Although a few researchers have concluded that this difference is due to _____ factors, most psychologists believe that the difference is due to _____ factors or to test _____.

racial (372)

15 (372)

heredity (372)
environmental (373); bias (373)

Mentally retarded individuals are those who have _____ intellectual functioning and also limitations in two or more _____ skill areas. About 90% of the mentally retarded are only _____ mentally retarded, with IQ scores in the _____ to 70 range. As adults, they are capable of _____ and functioning _____. 5%-10% of mentally retarded people are _____ mentally retarded, with IQs in the _____ to 50/55 range. These children are slow to develop _____ and _____ skills. They usually can progress to _____ grade academic material, and _____ require some supervision as adults. One's ability to function is drastically limited if one is either _____ retarded (those with IQs of about _____ to 40) or _____ retarded (those with IQs below ____). Most of these individuals are _____ for the majority of their lives.

subaverage (374)

adaptive (374)
mildly (375)
50 or 55 (375)
working (375); independently (375); moderately (375); 40 (375)
language (375); motor (375); 2nd (375)
will (375)
severely (375)
25 (375)
profoundly (375); 25 (375)
institutionalized (375)

_____ % of children are gifted or talented. Not only very bright children, but also those who are exceptionally _____ or _____, and those with strong _____ skills can be so designated. Although the stereotype of the gifted is that they are _____ adjusted and unpopular, the data suggests the opposite. One approach to accommodating gifted children is to _____ them; that is, to give them the same materials as other children but at a _____ pace. The other commonly used strategy is _____, in which children study topics at a greater _____ than their classmates.

3-5 (376)

creative (376); artistic (376), leadership (376)
poorly (376)

accelerate (376)
faster (376)
enrichment (376)
depth (376)

What can parents do to help their children succeed in school? First, they can frequently _____ to their children. They can _____ to them and get them to think about the world. They can provide a special place for children to _____. Finally, they can encourage their children's _____ skills.

read (377)
talk (377)

work (377)
problem-solving (377)

Crossword Puzzle

Cognitive Development In Middle Childhood

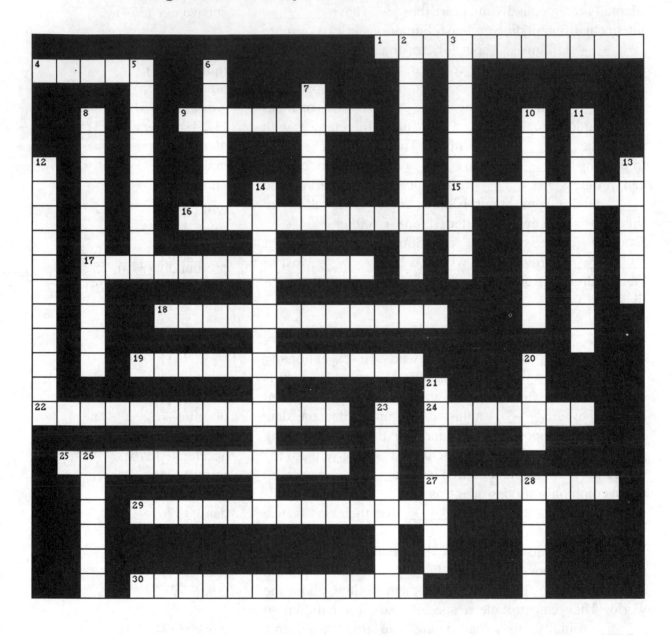

Across

1 The ability to take multiple aspects of a situation into account

4 Alfred _____, the developer of the first intelligence test

9 "IQ stands for "intelligence _____"

15 _____ retardation: having an IQ score of about 40 to 55

16 The capacity to think, problem-solve and understand the world

17 Programs that allow gifted children to move ahead at their own pace

18 Understandings of the causes behind others' behaviors

19 The use of more than one language

22 _____ age: one's actual age

24 Another term for "Black English"

25 The cultural _____ model is favored by those who view America as a melting pot.

27 _____-Binet Intelligence Scale

29 The goal of _____ education is to foster competence in both a child's minority culture and in the majority culture as well.

30 _____ intelligence is the store of information that a person has acquired

Down

2 The teacher _____ effect causes self-fulfilling prophecies in the classroom.

3 Programs in which gifted children are given activities to encourage a greater depth of study of grade-level material

5 Sternberg's _____ theory of intelligence

6 _____ Assessment Battery for Children (K-ABC)

7 _____ age: the intelligence level usual for people at a given age

8 Mental _____ is a subaverage level of intellectual functioning.

10 In _____ programs, all classes are taught in a foreign language.

11 An understanding of how one's own memory works

12 Believers in the _____ society model believe that persons should retain their separate ethnic identities.

13 The process by which information is recorded, stored, and retrieved

14 An understanding of one's own use of language

20 The abbreviation for Wechsler's adult intelligence test

21 _____ Intelligence Scale for Children-III

23 Piaget's _____ operational stage lasts from 7 to 12.

26 _____ retardation: having an IQ score in the range of 25 to 40

28 _____ intelligence is the ability to deal with new problems and situation.

Flash Cards

Name the four mental operations that emerge once concrete operations has been mastered.

What are the limitations of concrete operational thought?

What is wrong with preschoolers' understanding of the relationship between time and speed?

Why don't non-Western children enter concrete operations?

How does short term memory improve during middle childhood?

Give an example of a sentence written in the passive voice.

Give an example of a conditional sentence.

Which are the most difficult phonemes for children to say?

Why is metalinguistic awareness useful?

What are the benefits of being in a language immersion program?

Children cannot yet think abstractly, nor can they answer hypothetical questions.	Reversibility, identity, and compensation
They have not had the experiences that allow them to do so. They do have the capacity.	They think that two objects that arrive at the finish line at the same time must be traveling at the same speed (without taking distance into account).
John was kicked by Sarah.	The digit span becomes longer and it becomes more possible to manipulate the information.
J, v, th, and zh	If you help me now, I will buy you an ice cream cone later.
(1) Learn second language; (2) enhanced self-esteem; (3) cultural sensitivity; (4) cognitive benefits of being bilingual	Because children with metalinguistic awareness will ask for clarification.

What is the practical implication of believing Ebonics to be a separate language?

What rule of pragmatics emerges during elementary school?

What are the three "R's" of education?

How has public education changed in the 1990s?

Explain how Japanese and American attributional styles can affect student learning.

Why is it harmful to believe that external factors, such as luck, account for school success or failure?

List the four means by which teachers transmit their expectancies to students.

How do children's behaviors change if teachers have a high opinion of them?

Describe a self-fulfilling prophecy?

Why was the first intelligence test developed?

On which theory of intelligence was Binet's intelligence test based?

What is the formula for calculating a person's IQ?

That speakers should discuss the same topic	Children would be taught by teachers speaking Ebonics, at least in the early grades.
It emphasizes the basics more; there is more accountability, and it has become more multicultural.	Reading, wRiting, and aRithmetic
It is hard to be motivated to work hard if you believe that your level of success depends more on luck than on effort	Americans believe students fail due to lack of ability, the Japanese, due to lack of effort. Japanese students who fail are more encouraged to work harder.
They work harder and they develop higher self-esteem.	Via (1) the classroom socio-emotional climate; (2) differential feedback; (3) input to children; (4) output from teachers
In the early 20th century, the French government was interested in identifying those children who would have trouble in school.	The teacher has an initial low expectation and transmits it; the child is discouraged and fails; the teacher's view is confirmed and the cycle repeats.
Mental age/chronological age X 100	None. He devised his test empirically, by finding questions that distinguished bright from less-bright children.

Frieda is a 6-year old who is as bright as the average 8-year old. What is her IQ?

What is the advantage of using IQ scores rather than mental ages?

Name three IQ tests frequently given to children.

Are IQ tests good for anything?

List each of Gardner's seven aspects of intelligence.

Give an example of intrapersonal intelligence.

Give an example of interpersonal intelligence.

Give an example of musical intelligence.

What professions require a good deal of spatial intelligence?

List the three components of Sternberg's theory of intelligence.

How are IQ tests biased against the poor and people from minority groups?

What are Herrnstein's and Murray's controversial conclusions in *The Bell Curve*?

IQ scores let you compare the intelligence of people at different ages; mental age does not.	8/6 X 100 = 133
Yes. They are good at predicting how well children will do in school. They are not good at much else.	The Stanford-Binet, the WISC-III, and the K-ABC
Maria knows that she always reacts badly when her mother appears to favor her younger brother.	Musical, kinesthetic, logical-mathematical, linguistic, spatial, interpersonal, intrapersonal
Mozart composed his first symphony when he was seven years old.	Carlo is a great salesman: he knows just when to smile, just when to "push," just when to back-down when bargaining.
Componential, experiential, contextual	Navigator, architecture, artist, sculptor
They contend that racial differences in IQ are hereditary and the cause of racial inequities in poverty, and unemployment.	They require a good Standard English vocabulary in order to score well.

What is meant by "adaptive skill areas" in the definition of mental retardation?

What are the four sub-categories of mental retardation?

Mid (IQ = 55 to 70);
Moderate (IQ = 40 to 55);
Severe (IQ = 25 to 40);
Profound (IQ below 25)

Communication, self-care, home
living, social skills, community
use, self-direction, leisure
and work.

Practice Test One

1. When trying to decide which kind of candy to buy, seven-year old Juan notices that each piece of the red kind is bigger but you get more pieces of the green kind for the same amount of money. This is an example of
   a. reversibility.
   b. identity.
   c. conservation.
   d. decentering.

2. Which of the following statements is *false*?
   a. Piaget tended to overestimate elementary-schoolers' cognitive abilities.
   b. All children eventually master concrete operations.
   c. Decentering does not emerge until late in the concrete operational period.
   d. During middle childhood, children fail to take distance into account when judging speed.

3. Francine is enrolled in a French class in her school. In order to learn her vocabulary words, she thinks of the French word and pairs it with an English word that has a similar sound (though a different meaning). Francine is using
   a. Ebonics.
   b. the keyword approach.
   c. a control strategy.
   d. the immersion approach.

4. By 11 years of age, children have vocabularies of about
   a. 5000-10,000 words.
   b. 13,000-19,000 words.
   c. 20,000-27,000 words.
   d. 30,000-40,0000 words.

5. Which children do not tend to do well in language immersion programs?
   a. boys
   b. any child trying to learn a non-Western language
   c. immigrant or minority children
   d. majority children attempting to learn a minority language

6. Most linguists agree that
   a. Ebonics is not a variant of English but a separate language.
   b. Ebonics is a dialect of English.
   c. Ebonics is a degraded, inferior form of English.
   d. Ebonics is only trivially different from Standard English.

7. Which type of world citizen is least likely to be literate and have received an education?
   a. a female
   b. a Latin American
   c. a northern European
   d. an East Asian

8. Which of the following is *least* influential in determining school readiness?
   a. a child's overall maturity level
   b. a child's parents' attitudes towards school and reading
   c. a child's age relative to his/her classmates
   d. the educational level of a child's parents

9. How does American education in the 1990s differ from American education in the 1970s and 1980s?
   a. Students are less likely to take proficiency tests.
   b. Students are more likely to follow a set curriculum.
   c. Students are less likely to receive a multicultural education.
   d. Teachers are less likely to be held accountable for their students' successes or failures.

10. Paul believes in the ideal of the American melting pot. He welcomes immigration, but believes that all immigrants should learn English and adopt "American" culture. He would support
    a. the cultural assimilation model.   c. the pluralistic society model.
    b. monocultural education.   d. fostering bicultural identities.

11. Mr. Kaye has been told that one of his new students, Magda, has been having trouble doing well in her old school. Mr. Kaye will most likely
    a. not alter his behavior towards her.
    b. give her extra encouragement and support.
    c. give her harder work to help her catch up.
    d. spend less time interacting with her.

12. The first IQ test was specifically designed to
    a. predict how well adults could handle demanding jobs.
    b. identify extremely intellectually gifted children .
    c. predict how well children would succeed in school.
    d. screen for mental retardation in army draftees.

13. Maia is 9 years old, and she functions at a 6-year-old intellectual level. What is her IQ?
    a. 6
    b. 9
    c. 67
    d. 133

14. Which of the following IQ tests is the most flexible?
    a. the Stanford-Binet
    b. the K-ABC
    c. the WAIS-III
    d. the WISC-III

15. Which of the theories of intelligence contains, in part, an aspect of intelligence that is similar to "common sense?"
   a. Vygotsky's approach
   b. the fluid vs. crystallized approach
   c. Gardner's approach
   d. Sternberg's approach

16. Which of the following contributes *least* to racial differences in IQ?
   a. poverty and socio-economic issues
   b. test bias
   c. heredity
   d. social factors

17. Which mentally retarded individuals can likely hold down jobs and live independently on their own?
   a. mildly mentally retarded individuals
   b. mildly and moderately retarded individuals
   c. mildly, moderately and severely retarded individuals
   d. Almost no mentally retarded individuals are capable of living independently on their own.

18. Jeremy is a gifted child. At 9, he has already completed high school math and is ready to move on to calculus. Which is probably true about Jeremy?
   a. He is socially maladjusted and unpopular.
   b. He is a poor athlete.
   c. He is very healthy.
   d. He is nervous and a little neurotic.

19. What should parents do if they wish to maximize their child's chances of success in school?
   a. Read to them.
   b. Help them solve problems on their own.
   c. Give them a quiet place to work.
   d. all of the above

Test Solutions

Self-Quiz Solution

1. d (page 345)
2. a (page 346)
3. b (page 349)
4. b (page 350)
5. c (page 353)
6. b (page 353)
7. a (page 355)
8. c (page 356)
9. b (page 356)
10. a (page 358

11. d (page 363)
12. c (page 366)
13. c (page 367)
14. b (page 368)
15. d (page 371)
16. c (page 373)
17. a (page 375)
18. c (page 376)
19. d (page 377)

Crossword Puzzle Solution

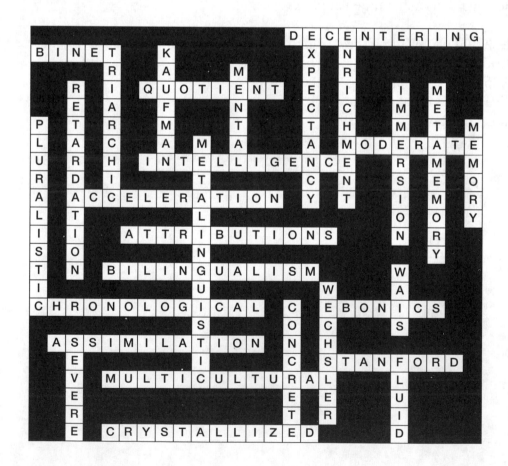

CHAPTER 12

Social and Personality Development in Middle Childhood

INTERESTING AND IMPORTANT THINGS YOU'LL KNOW AFTER READING THIS CHAPTER...

1. Which children are most likely to be aggressive? See page 388.

2. Do African-American children have lower self-esteem than Caucasian children? See page 389.

3. What makes some children popular when others are not? See page 393.

4. How are boys' friendships different than girls'? See page 396.

5. How well do children fare after a divorce? See page 401. After a remarriage? See page 402.

THE DEVELOPING SELF

Understanding one's self: A new response to "Who am I?"

Psychosocial development in middle childhood: Industry vs. Inferiority

Self-esteem: Developing a positive – or negative – view of oneself

Self-esteem, violence, and aggression: The downside of high self-esteem

Self-efficacy: Expecting to be capable

RELATIONSHIPS: BUILDING FRIENDSHIP IN MIDDLE CHILDHOOD

Stages of friendship: Changing views of friends

Status among school-age children: Establishing a pecking order

Individual differences in friendship: What makes a child popular?

Gender and friendship: The sex segregation of middle childhood

Promoting friendships across racial and ethnic lines: Integration in and out of the classroom

Increasing children's social competence

FAMILY LIFE

Families in the 1990s: The changing world of family life

The consequences of group care: Orphanages in the 1990s

Learning Objectives

When you have mastered the material in this chapter, you should be able to ...

1. Explain how children's self-concepts change during middle childhood and how social comparisons affect these self-concepts. (page 384)

2. Describe the psychosocial stage of industry vs. inferiority. (page 386)

3. Discuss the importance of self-esteem and describe how it changes during middle childhood. (page 386)

4. Characterize the relationship between self-esteem and aggression. (page 388)

5. Discuss how and under what circumstances ethnicity affects self-esteem. (page 388)

6. Discuss the factors that influence the development of self-efficacy. (page 389)

7. Enumerate the benefits children derive from having friends. (page 391)

8. Summarize Damon's view of the development of friendship. (page 391)

9. Contrast the friendships and social interactions of high- and low-status children. (page 392)

10. Compare the characteristics of popular, neglected, and rejected children and know the consequences of being popular, neglected, and rejected. (page 393)

11. Outline Dodge's model of social problem solving. (page 395)

12. Describe gender differences in friendships during middle childhood. (page 396)

13. Explain how to foster cross-racial friendships. (page 397)

14. Describe steps that can be taken to help children develop social competence. (page 399)

15. Describe both the short-term and the longer-term effects of divorce on children. (page 401)

16. Discuss the role ambiguity and other issues that typify blended families. (page 402)

17. Explain the effects on children of having two working parents. (page 402.

18. Comment on the data concerning the welfare of self-care children. (page 403)

19. Describe the issues that affect the quality of the experiences of children in single-parent families. (page 403)

20. Describe the children who are served in group homes. (page 404)

Guided Review

The Developing Self

During middle childhood, children come to view themselves less in terms of _____ attributes and more in terms of _____ traits. In addition, their self-concepts become increasingly _____. In particular, they become divided into physical, _____, _____, and academic realms. Children in part develop their self concepts by making social _____, usually measuring themselves against _____ individuals. In order to bolster their self-esteem, some children make _____ social comparisons.

external (384)
psychological (384)
differentiated (384)
social (384); emotional (384)

comparisons(385)
similar (385)
downward (385)

During middle childhood, children pass through Erickson's industry vs. _____ stage. At this time, they learn the value of _____. Children who experience too much failure at this time may withdraw, both _____ and _____. A recent study suggests that industriousness in childhood is a _____ trait, and carries over into adulthood, where it is predictive of _____.

inferiority (386)
mastery (386)
academically (386)
socially (386)
stable (386)
success (386)

_____ refers to one's feelings about one's own worth. It is based upon comparisons with _____ and with one's own _____. Self-esteem becomes more _____ during middle childhood and it tends to _____ until 12. Then it dips, largely due to _____ transition. Low self-esteem can set up a cycle of _____. New data, however, suggests that many children who are _____ have unreasonably _____ self-esteem. This leads to _____ when their self-views are challenged.

Self-esteem (386)
others (386)
standards (386); differentiated (386); increase (386)
school (386)
failure (386)
aggressive (388)
high (388); anger (388)

For many years it was believed that members of minority groups would have _____ self-esteem than members of majority groups. Now that societal views about the _____ of discrimination have changed, differences between minority and majority self-esteem levels have _____.

lower (388)

inevitability (389)

decreased (389)

_____ refers to one's belief that he or she can do something well. It is critical to success because it _____ effort and _____. Self-efficacy levels are influenced by prior success or _____, observation of _____ performance, and by _____.

Self-efficacy (389)
motivates (390)
persistence (390)
failure (390); others' (390)
reinforcement (390)

peer (391)

information (391); emotional (391); social (391)

3 (391); 7- (391)
like (391)
time (391); activities (391); 8 and 10 (391); personal (392)
responsive (392)
trust (392)

intimacy (392); loyalty (392)
exclusive (392)

Status (392)

similar (392); more (392)
exclusive (393)
activity (393)

competence (393)
cooperative (393); funny (393); nonverbal (393); dependent (394); immature (394); aggressive (394); shy (394)
unattractive (394)

Neglected (394)
academically (394); happy (394) incompetent (394)
disliked (394); competence (394); poorly (395)

problem-solving (395)

identify (395) interpret (395)
determine (395)
evaluate (395); select (395)
enact (395)
taught (396)

During middle childhood, children become increasingly involved with their _____ group. Friendships are important to development, since friends can provide _____ and _____ support and they allow children to practice _____ skills.

According to William Damon, friendship passes through _____ stages. Four to _____ year olds view friends as people who _____ them and with whom they spend _____ and do _____. Between _____, children begin to take others' _____ qualities into account and they begin to prefer friends who are _____ to them. The mainstay of stage two friendship is mutual _____. During late middle childhood, the qualities most valued in friends are _____ and _____, and friendships become more _____.

_____ differences become more pronounced during middle childhood. Children tend to be friends with others of _____ status. High-status children tend to have _____ friends, and to form more _____ friendships. In general, they spend more time engaged in social _____.

Popular children tend to have high social _____. They are _____, _____, and are good at reading others' _____ behavior. They are not overly _____. Unpopular children may be _____ or overly _____ or excessively _____. They are more likely than popular children to be physically _____.

_____ children are ignored by their peers. These children tend to do well _____, and to be _____ (although they do view themselves as socially _____). Rejected children are _____ because they lack social _____. They are more likely to grow up _____ adjusted.

Popularity is also influenced by social _____ skills. In order to know how to behave in a given social situation, a child must first _____ social cues, and then _____ those cues. He must then _____ possible responses, _____ those responses and then _____ the best. Finally, he must _____ that response. Fortunately, children can be _____ these skills.

During middle childhood, most children _____ themselves by sex. Boys usually have _____ social networks than girls and they spend more time playing in _____. They tend to have rigid _____ hierarchies and to be concerned with their _____ in that hierarchy. This leads to _____ play. Girls tend to have one or two _____ and they avoid _____ differences. Girls are more likely to _____ with their friends. This gender segregation is _____ to many cultures.

segregate (396)
larger (396)
groups (396)
dominant (396)
place (396)
restrictive (396); best friends (397); status (397)
compromise (397)
common (397)

As children age, their number of cross-racial friendships _____. African-American children are _____ likely than Caucasian children to name a cross-race best friend. Contact between children of different races is beneficial in that it helps them perceive _____, it reduces _____, and lets children know others as _____. The most effective contacts involve children of _____ statuses who are working _____ together.

decrease (397); less (398)

commonalities (398); biases (398); individuals (398)
equal (398)
cooperatively (398)

Social competence can be encouraged by providing children with _____ opportunities. Parents can also teach _____ and _____ skills. Children can be made aware of the importance of _____ communication.

social (399)
listening (399); conversation (399); nonverbal (399)

Family Life

No matter what type of family they live in, children and their parents _____ the child's behavior during middle childhood. That is, the parents set down broad _____ for behavior, and the children control their _____ activities.

coregulate (401)
guidelines (401)
day-to-day (401)

For up to _____ after a divorce, children show signs of stress. In particular, they may be _____, _____ or develop _____ disturbances. Younger children feel _____ and responsible for the divorce; older children feel pressured to _____. Most children adjust after this initial period of upset, but _____ as many children whose parents have divorced need _____ than those from intact homes. Several factors influence the ultimate effects the divorce has on children. One is the _____ standing of the parents after the divorce. Second is the _____ the children retain with the non-custodial parent. Third is the degree of _____ that existed in the home prior to the divorce. (It is _____ stressful to experience a divorce than to live in a hostile household.

2 years (401)
anxious (401); depressed (401); sleep (401)
guilty (401)
take sides (401)
twice (401)
counseling (401)

economic (401)

relationship (401)
hostility (401)
more (401)

blended (402)
ambiguity (402)
happier (402); may not (402)
better (402)

economic (402)
chores (402)
interact (402)

well (402)
satisfied (403); nurturing (403)

do not (403)

self-care (403)

lonely (403)

unsupervised (403); peers (403)

25% (403)
increasing (403)
more (403)

never married (404)

economic (404)
present (404); relationship
(404)

group (404)
treatment (404)
smaller (404)

increased (405)
abused (405); neglected (405);
25% (405)
10 (405)

emotional (405)

With the high divorce rate comes an increase in the number of _____ families. Children in these families often experience role _____. Therefore, even though parents are often _____ after remarriage, their children _____ be. School-age children typically fare _____ than adolescents in blended family situations, in part because the family's _____ standing improves and in part because there are more persons with whom to share _____ and with whom to _____.

Children in families in which both parents are employed usually fare quite _____. This may be because parents who are _____ with their lives tend to be more _____ towards their children. Also, children whose parents both work outside the home _____ spend less time interacting with their parents than children who have one or more unemployed parents.

Some children — called _____ children — are left to fend for themselves after school. Although these children sometimes report being _____, they are no less well-adjusted than their peers. In fact, staying home by oneself may be safer than spending _____ time with _____.

Almost _____ of American children live with only one parent, and this percentage is _____. Minority children are _____ likely to spend time in a single-parent family than majority children. The most common type of single-parent family involves a woman who _____ and her children. Factors that determine the success of this family situation include _____ status, whether a second parent was _____ earlier, and the previous _____ between the two parents.

The term *orphanage* has been replaced with "_____ home" and "residential _____ center." These facilities usually house a _____ number of children than in the past. The number of children living in these facilities has _____ dramatically. The majority of the children who live in group homes have been _____ and _____. About _____ of the children placed in group homes stay there indefinitely. Group-home care is about ____ times as costly as foster care. Children in these homes fare best when they form a close _____ relationship with one of the home's workers.

Crossword Puzzle

Social and Personality Development During Middle Childhood

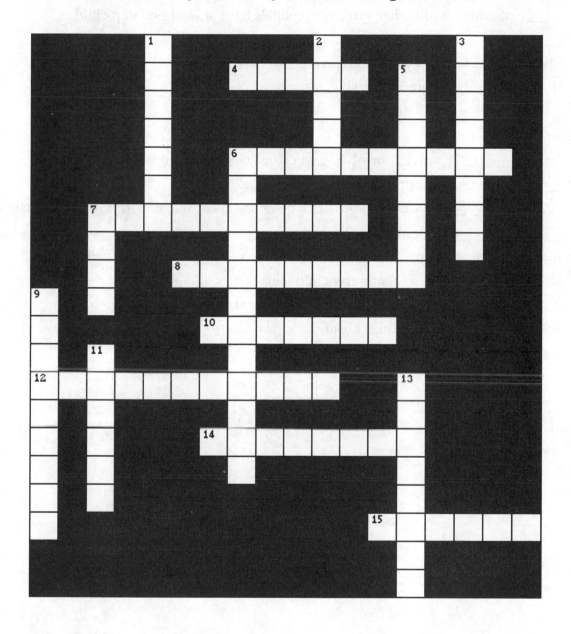

Across

4   Persons who are about your same age

6   Social _____: the collection of skills that allow a person to successfully operate in a social situation

7   Social _____: the desire to evaluate one's own abilities against those of others

8   _____ children receive little attention

10 _____ families result when remarried couples have at least one step-child.

12 _____ treatment centers: a modern synonym for orphanages

14 Making these social comparisons protects self-esteem

15 How others in your group rate you

Down

1   Social _____ solving involves using strategies for solving social conflicts.

2   _____ home: a modern synonym for orphanage

3   Self-_____: one's expectations that he or she is capable of carrying out a behavior

5   _____ children are actively disliked.

6   A transitional stage in which both parents and child control a child's behavior

7   Self-_____ children let themselves into their homes after school.

9   A dominance _____ represents the relative status of those in a group.

11 Self-_____: one's feelings about one's own worth

13 _____ vs. inferiority

Flash Cards

Describe two ways that self-concept changes during middle childhood.	What are the four domains of children's self-concepts?
What is "social reality?"	Why do some children choose to make downward social comparisons?
Contrast the terms "self-concept" and "self-esteem."	How does self-esteem change during middle childhood?
What do we mean when we say that self-concept and self-esteem become more differentiated?	Give an example of the "cycle of failure" associated with low self-esteem.
How can high self-esteem lead to aggression?	Describe Kenneth Clark's pioneering study on race and self esteem.

Academic, physical, social, and emotional	It becomes more based upon psychological traits and it becomes more differentiated (rather than global).
Because it bolsters their self-esteem (since they look good compared to those they are comparing themselves with)	Understanding that is derived from how others think about and view the world.
It increases through age 12 and becomes more differentiated.	Self-concept, refers to ones beliefs about the self; self-esteem refers to how one emotionally feels about the self.
Jay thinks he will fail a test because he thinks he's dumb, so he doesn't bother to study, so he fails, which confirms his low opinion of himself.	We mean that children come to know they are good at some things but not others. Younger children think they are, overall, good or bad.
He asked children to choose dolls that were "good" or "nice." Black children in the 1940s selected the white dolls.	They are easily angered by challenges to their self-esteem, which must come often because they are irrationally inflated.

Which does a child have fewer of: peers or friends?

Characterize each of Damon's three stages of friendship.

What do children dislike in each other?

Contrast neglected and rejected children.

Are rejected children disliked because they have behavioral problems, or do they have behavioral problems because they are rejected?

Using Dodge's model, what makes some children popular?

Specifically describe interventions that have been found to help unpopular children.

What is "border work?"

How does restrictive play affect the pace of boys' play interactions?

Discuss the situations in which girls are apt to be confrontational.

Contrast the language used by pairs of male and female friends during middle childhood.

Under what circumstances is prejudice most likely to be reduced?

(1) Pleasant times; (2) trust; (3) loyalty and intimacy	Friends
Neglected children are ignored, but not disliked; rejected children are actively disliked. Rejected children are less happy.	Aggression, anger, dishonesty, critical behavior, greed, teasing, unfaithfulness
They are better at detecting and interpreting social cues, and they have a larger repertoire of responses from which to choose.	We don't know.
The term describes the brief forays that children make into cross-sex (enemy) territory.	Teaching disclosure, to ask questions, to offer suggestions, and to decode facial expressions
When they interact with boys or with girls who aren't friends. They are not confrontational with friends (unlike boys).	It makes them more choppy and interrupted.
When children are of equal status, when they work cooperatively together, and when tolerance is emphasized	Boys issue commands whereas girls make indirect requests.

Describe three ways that current American families differ from those of previous generations.

What percentage of American children spend their entire childhoods living with both of their biological parents?

What three factors influence how well children adjust to their parents' divorce?

Under what circumstance do children appear to benefit from their parents' divorce?

Describe one of the common problems of blended family life.

How much less time do parents in families where both parents are employed spend with their children compared to parents in families where mom stays home?

What factors influence the success of single-parent families?

Why do most children who live in group homes end up there?

What does the acronym SODAS stand for?

About 50%	More children will experience divorce, be in blended families, and be raised by a single parent.
In those families in which there was a lot of hostility and fighting between the parents before the divorce	Their economic situation, the nature of their parents' relationship prior to the divorce, the quality of relationships with their parents after the divorce.
Essentially no less time	Role ambiguity: no one knows how to behave toward their step-relations
Because they were abused or neglected	The families' economic standing, the degree of stress in the household, the amount of time the parent can spend with the child
	Situation, Options, Disadvantages, Advantages, Solution

Practice Test One

1. Dylan has just had his eleventh birthday. How is his self-concept likely to be different than it was when he was 6?
   a. It is more global.
   b. It is more based upon sports and physical prowess.
   c. It is more based upon comparisons with others.
   d. It is less positive.

2. The psychosocial stage that occurs during middle childhood is
   a. industry vs. inferiority.
   b. autonomy vs. shame.
   c. initiative vs. guilt.
   d. identity vs. diffusion.

3. Why does children's self-esteem take a dip towards the end of middle childhood?
   a. because of the transition to middle school
   b. because of self-comparisons with children who have already reached puberty
   c. because children become more physically awkward at this time
   d. because children are losing interest in many activities that they formerly enjoyed

4. According to the most recent research, which children are apt to be aggressive?
   a. children with very low levels of self-esteem
   b. children with moderately low levels of self-esteem
   c. children with fairly high self-esteem
   d. children with unreasonably high levels of self-esteem

5. The self-esteem of African-American children
   a. has decreased steadily since the 1940s.
   b. has remained fairly stable since the 1940s.
   c. increased during the 1960s and 1970s but begun to drop again in the 1990s.
   d. has increased to near majority levels.

6. Nina has a very high level of self-efficacy. This means she will probably
   a. be aggressive.
   b. be motivated to work hard.
   c. like herself.
   d. attribute success to external factors.

7. Friends don't
   a. provide children with information about other people.
   b. help children learn how to handle their own emotions.
   c. foster intellectual growth.
   d. provide frequent contacts with non-peers.

8. Harrison describes his best friend this way: "He helps me when I'm in trouble. He sometimes shares his best baseball cards with me. He let me borrow his bike when mine was broken." Harrison is probably about
   a. 4-6 years old.
   b. 6-8 years old.
   c. 8-10 years old.
   d. 10-12 years old.

9. Yolanda enjoys high status among her peers. Which is probably *not* true of Yolanda?
   a. She plays with younger children.
   b. She has many friends.
   c. She is in a clique.
   d. Many children consider her a friend.

10. Warner is a neglected child. Which of the following statements about him is most likely true?
    a. He is very lonely.
    b. He is a poor student academically.
    c. He is aggressive.
    d. He sees himself as fairly well accepted.

11. Which is the first step in Dodge's model of social problem-solving?
    a. Devise a variety of possible responses.
    b. Select the best response.
    c. Identify social cues.
    d. Interpret social cues.

12. Jeff and Jill are 10-year-old twins. Which of the following is probably true of their friendships?
    a. Jill has more friends than Jeff.
    b. Jeff is more competitive with his friends than Jill.
    c. Jill orders her friends around more than Jeff.
    d. Jill is more likely to engage in restrictive play with her friends.

13. If you were the principal of a newly integrated school, which might you do to foster cross-racial friendships?
    a. Leave the children alone to work things out for themselves.
    b. Pit the children of the difference races against each other in team sports and contests.
    c. Encourage the students to work together to solve mutual problems.
    d. Make sure that each class had equal numbers of students of all races.

14. Which of the following does not enhance children's social competence?
    a. letting children pick their own teams
    b. signing children up for organized activities, such as team sports
    c. teaching children to use "I" statements
    d. teaching children to be good listeners

15. Lisette's parents have just informed her that they are going to get a divorce. Lisette will most likely
    a. have a very hard 6 months, and then bounce back.
    b. have a very hard year or two, and then bounce back.
    c. develop disruptive behaviors and emotional problems that will plague her throughout childhood.
    d. experience little difficulty, and behave much as before.

16. Which child will most likely adjust most readily to living in a blended family?
    a. Jean, a 10-year old
    b. Darlene, a 12-year old
    c. Maggie, a 14-year old
    d. Juanita, a 16-year old

17. Which mother is most likely to raise well-adjusted children?
    a. One who is a full-time homemaker.
    b. One who works part-time outside the home.
    c. One who works full-time outside the home.
    d. Whichever mother is most satisfied with her life.

18. Self-care children who stay home alone after school are more likely to
    a. be harmed in an accident than other children.
    b. be molested by an adult than other children.
    c. develop emotional problems than other children.
    d. none of the above

19. Ameka is an African American 8-year old. He most likely lives
    a. only with his mother, who is divorced.
    b. only with his mother, who never married.
    c. in a household with both of his biological parents.
    d. in a blended household, with his mother and her new husband.

20. Placing a child in a group home
    a. is much more expensive than placing him in foster care.
    b. is somewhat more expensive than placing her in foster care.
    c. costs about the same as placing him in foster care.
    d. costs considerably less than placing her in foster care.

Test Solutions

Self-Quiz Solution

1. c (page 384)
2. a (page 386)
3. a (page 387)
4. d (page 388)
5. d (page 389)
6. b (page 390)
7. d (page 391)
8. c (page 392)
9. a (page 392)
10. d (page 394)

11. c. (page 395)
12. b (page 396)
13. c (page 398)
14. a (page 399)
15. b (page 401)
16. a (page 402)
17. d (page 403)
18. d (page 403)
19. b (page 403)
20. a (page 405

Crossword Puzzle Solution

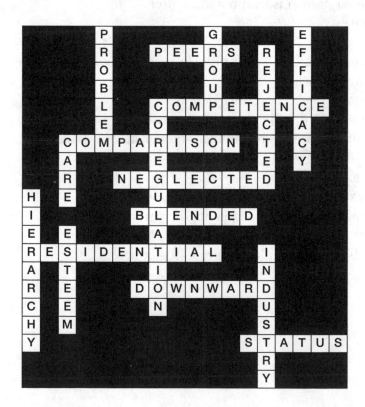

CHAPTER 13

Physical Development in Adolescence

INTERESTING AND IMPORTANT THINGS YOU'LL KNOW AFTER READING THIS CHAPTER...

1. How do most teens feel about experiencing puberty? See page 418.

2. If a child had a choice in the matter, should he or she choose to be an early-maturer or a late-boomer? See page 419.

3. Has your life been so stressful recently that you are at risk? See page 426.

4. Is adolescent drug use becoming more or less common? See page 430.

5. What are the leading causes of death among American teens? See page 435.

6. How can you tell if a friend is using drugs? See page 439.

PHYSICAL MATURATION

Growth during adolescence: The rapid pace of physical and sexual maturation

Nutrition and food: Fueling the growth of adolescence

Anorexia nervosa and bulimia: The frightening world of eating disorders

STRESS AND COPING

The origins of stress: Reacting to life's challenges

The consequences of stress: Physical and psychological wear and tear

Coping with stress: Meeting the challenges of stress

Coping with stress

THREATS TO ADOLESCENTS' WELL-BEING

Illegal drugs

Alcohol: Use and abuse

Tobacco: The dangers of smoking

Selling death: Pushing smoking to the less advantaged

Dying in adolescence: The risk of death

Sexually transmitted diseases: One cost of sex

Hooked on drugs or alcohol?

Learning Objectives

When you have mastered the material in this chapter, you should be able to ...

1. Describe the sequence of events – including both the adolescent growth spurt and those directly involved with sexual maturation – that occurs during adolescence. (page 416)

2. Discuss the psychological effects of undergoing puberty. (page 418)

3. Explain how early or late physical maturation affects both girls and boys. (page 419)

4. Describe the symptoms and causes of the three adolescent eating disorders: obesity, anorexia nervosa, and bulimia. (page 421)

5. Understand the cognitive component of stress. (page 424)

6. Explain the kinds of experiences that produce stress. (page 425)

7. Describe the physical consequences of stress. (page 425)

8. Delineate the four coping styles that can be used to neutralize stress. (page 427)

9. Advise someone about possible stress-reduction strategies. (page 427)

10. Contrast drug use in the mid-1990s with drug use in the the 1970s, 1980s, and early 1990s. (page 430)

11. Compare the types of addiction and understand the dangers of drug use. (page 431)

12. Understand the patterns, causes, and risks of using alcohol. (page 431)

13. Explain the reasons that teenagers smoke cigarettes, even when they are aware of the health risks of doing so. (page 432)

14. Cite the main reasons for adolescent death, and know which teens are particularly at risk. (page 435)

15. Describe the symptoms of AIDs and several other sexually transmitted diseases, and be able to describe ways to prevent infection. (page 436)

16. Outline some of the warning signs of drug abuse. (page 439)

Guided Review

Physical Maturation

Physical change during adolescence is extremely _____. During the growth _____, teenagers usually put on between _____ inches per year in height. In girls, this growth usually begins at about _____; In boys, it begins _____ later.

rapid (416)
spurt (416)
3-5 (416)
10 (416)
two years (416)

_____, the period of sexual maturation, similarly begins about two years _____ in girls, beginning at about _____. Pubertal changes are caused by increased levels of _____ and _____ in the adolescents' bodies. _____, the first menstrual period, begins later in girls who are _____ and earlier in girls who are under _____. During the past one hundred years, the age at which girls begin to menstruate has _____, an example of a _____ trend. (This trend has now _____.)

Puberty (416)
earlier (416)
11 or 12 (416)
estrogens (417); androgens (417); Menarche (417)
malnourished (417)
stress (417)
decreased (417)
secular (417); ceased (418)

Adolescents' bodies change in numerous ways. Some of these changes involve _____ sex characteristics; these are changes that directly affect the reproductive organs. Other changes involve _____ sex characteristics, and affect those body parts that signify sexual maturation but are not directly involved in reproduction (e.g., pubic and _____ hair).

primary (418)

secondary (418)

underarm (418)

Girls usually react to menarche with increased self-_____ and self-_____. Girls are _____ to discuss menstruation with their mothers, but boys rarely mention their first _____ to anyone. Adolescents frequently react to their changing bodies with _____. Girls tend to be particularly _____, especially because most are putting down extra _____ at this time.

esteem (418)
awareness (418); likely (419)

ejaculation (419)
embarrassment (419)
unhappy (419)
fat (419)

Early maturation is largely _____ for boys, who become _____ and more _____. Although there may be short-term problems (such as with _____), usually these boys become successful adults. Early-maturing girls have a more _____ time. They become very _____ about their bodies and suffer from _____. In other countries, such as _____, these negative effects _____ so pronounced.

positive (419)
popular (419); athletic (419)
delinquency (419)

difficult (420); self-conscious (420); teasing (420)
Germany (420); are not (420)

boys (420)
girls (420); athletes (420)
short (420)
low (420)
esteem (420)
slender (420)

increases (421)
calcium (421)
iron (421)
5% (421); 15% (421)

nervosa (421)
15-20% (421)
white (421) girls (421)
fat (421)
Bulimia (421)
binging (421)
girls (421)

depression (421); heart (421)

biological (421); environmental (421)
slenderness (421)

threaten (424); challenge (424)
positive (424)
blood pressure (424)
sweating (424)
negative (424)
illness (424)
circulatory (424)

primary (424)

secondary (424)
resources (424); abilities (424)

threatening (424); unable (424)
Negative (425); uncontrollable (425); ambiguous (425)

Late-maturation is more of a problem for _____ than for _____. Late-maturing boys are relatively poor _____ and are perceived as too _____. Before they have matured late-blooming girls may have ____ status, but once they reach puberty their self-_____ becomes high, probably because late-maturing girls are apt to be _____.

Food intake _____ sharply during adolescence. It is important that they ingest enough _____ to ensure good bone growth and enough _____ to prevent anemia. About _____ of adolescents are obese, and another _____ are less extremely overweight. A phobia about gaining weight can lead to anorexia _____, an extremely serious disorder with a _____ death rate. This disorder most often strikes _____, affluent adolescent _____. A part of this syndrome is that anorexics see themselves as _____, even though they have become skeletally thin. _____ is a disorder characterized by _____ and purging. It, too, primarily affects adolescent _____. Although most bulimics do not become emaciated, they may suffer from _____, and in extreme cases, _____ failure. There are conflicting theories as to the cause of eating disorders, but both _____ and _____ factors are considered important. In particular, these disorders appear only in cultures that emphasize female _____.

Stress and Coping

Stress results when events _____ or _____ us. Even _____ experiences can generate stress. Although the body's emergency reaction to stress — increased _____, _____, etc. — can be helpful in the short run, it has _____ long-term consequences. For example, chronically-stressed individuals are more susceptible to _____ and may develop _____ problems.

According to Richard Lazarus, _____ appraisal involves examining a situation in order to determine whether it is harmful. This is followed by _____ appraisal, an evaluation of one's own _____ and _____. In order for an experience to produce stress, one must conclude both that it is _____ and that one will likely be _____ to cope with it. _____ and _____ events are more likely to cause stress than those that are not. _____ demands are particularly draining.

Physical reactions to chronic stress include _____ and _____ aches, rashes, _____, and susceptibility to illness. Psychosomatic disorders, such as _____, asthma, and _____ pressure may develop as well.

head (425)
back (425); fatigue (425)
ulcers (426)
high blood (426)

There are three main styles of _____ with stress. _____-focused coping means tackling the problem _____. _____-focused coping involves consciously regulating one's feelings about the stressor. Both of these are superior to _____ coping, which consists of _____ reality by _____ the problem and solves nothing.

coping (427)
Problem (427)
head-on (427); Emotion (427)

defensive (427); distorting (427); trivializing (427)

Good ways to deal with stress include seeking _____ over the situation, _____ the stressor as less threatening, seeking social _____, using _____ techniques, and remembering that stress is a _____ part of life.

control (427)
reappraising (427)
support (427); relaxation (427)
normal (427)

Threats to Adolescents' Well-Being

Almost _____ of American high school seniors have experimented with illegal drugs at least once. Use of illegal drugs has _____ since the late 1980s and early 1990s, although it is still lower than it was in the _____. Disapproval of occasional marijuana use is _____.

half (430)

increased (430)
1970s (430)
decreasing (430)

Adolescents use drugs for many reasons. Some do it simply for the _____ it brings; others do it to escape from the _____ of their lives or for the thrill of doing something _____. Some are motivated by _____ pressure.

pleasure (431)
stresses (431)
illegal (431); peer (431)

Many illegal drugs are _____. _____ addictive drugs change the body so that it cannot function in their _____. Drugs that are _____ addictive make people believe that they cannot _____ without the drug. Drugs are dangerous because they help people _____ confronting and solving their real problems.

addictive (431); Biologically (431); absence (431)
psychologically (431)
cope (431)
avoid (431)

_____ of college students report having had at least one drink during the past 30 days; more than _____ claim to have had more than 5 drinks in the past two weeks. Particularly disturbing is the high rate of _____ drinking — ____ drinks at one sitting for men and _____ drinks at one sitting for women — that occurs. One study indicated that _____ of college men and _____ of college women had binged during the past two weeks. Binge drinkers not only put themselves at risk, but they _____ others by their disruptive behavior.

3/4 (431)
40% (431)

binge (431)
5 (431); 4 (431)

50% (431); 39% (431)

annoy and endanger (431)

adults (431); tension (431)
inhibitions (431); diminishes
(431); judgment (431); 1/3
(431); cannot (431)

identify (439)
magazines (439)
deterioration (439)
lapses (439); concentrating
(439); decline (439); absent
(439); dishonesty (439)
hostility (439); secretiveness
(439); friends (439); extra-cur-
ricular (439)
declining (432); Girls (432)
more (432)
cool (434)
nicotine (434)
biologically (434)
psychologically (434)
foreign countries (435)

are not (435)
Accidents (435); car (435)
more (435)
Homicide (436)
Suicide (436)
three (436)

immunodeficiency (436)
minorities (436); Everyone
(437)
invulnerable (437)

sexually (437) 1/4 (437)

chlamydia (437)
antibiotics (437)
burning (437)
discharge (437); herpes (438);
viral (438); incurable (438);
blisters (438)
trichmoniasis (438); gonorrhea
(438); Syphillis (438)

Adolescents turn to alcohol because it makes them feel like _____, and because it reduces _____ and _____. Unfortunately, alcohol also _____ one's driving ability and impairs _____. Perhaps _____ of adolescents are alcoholics – persons who _____ control their drinking behavior.

There are numerous warning signs that an adolescent is involved in drug use. First, they may appear to _____ with the drug culture; e.g., they may own drug-related _____. They may show signs of physical _____ or have memory _____ and difficulty in _____. Their school performance may _____ and they may begin to be frequently _____ from school. Their behavior may change to include _____, _____ and _____. They may change _____ and lose interest in _____ activities.

Overall, smoking among teenagers is _____. _____, however, are _____ likely to drink than in the past. Teens smoke in good part because it is _____ to do so. Once they have begun, they continue because _____, the active chemical ingredient in cigarettes is both _____ and _____ addictive. In order to maintain their profitability, tobacco companies have begun targeting teens in _____.

Most adolescent deaths _____ the result of natural causes. _____, primarily _____ accidents, are the leading cause of adolescent death. Teenage boys are _____ likely to die than teenage girls. _____ is now the second leading cause of death among older adolescents. _____, the third leading cause of death, has become _____ times as frequent in the past 30 years.

Death from AIDS, or acquired _____ disorder, is also on the rise, particularly among _____. _____ who contracts the HIV virus ultimately dies. Adolescents tend to feel _____, and this allows them to engage in risky behavior. This not only increases their chances to contract AIDs, but also other _____ transmitted diseases. In fact, _____ of American teens contracts an STD before graduating from high school! The most common STD is _____. Fortunately it can be treated with _____. Symptoms may include a _____ sensation while urinating and a _____. Genital _____ is _____, like AIDs, and, like AIDs is _____. Symptoms consist of small _____ around the genitals. Three other of the most common STDs are _____, _____, and _____.

Crossword Puzzle

Physical Development in Adolescence

Across

2   The response to events that threaten or challenge us

5   During the growth _____, adolescents grow 3-4" per year.

6   _____ sex characteristic; e.g., having a scrotum

7   People who are addicted to alcohol

9   Secondary _____ involves deciding whether one's coping abilities are adequate.

10 The most common STD

14 _____ coping involves distorting reality.

17 _____ nervosa

18 Short for "sexually transmitted disease"

19 The "binge-purge" eating disorder

20 AIDS: Acquired _____ Syndrome

Down

1   The period of sexual maturation

2   _____ support is given to us by others.

3   The _____ trend

4   The effort to control, reduce, or learn to tolerate the threats that lead to stress

6   _____ disorders include ulcers and high blood pressure.

8   Genital _____, an STD caused by a virus

9   The developmental stage between childhood and adulthood

11 Describes a drug that produces a biological or psychological dependency

12 _____ sex characteristic; e.g., having pubic hair

13 A girl's first menstrual period

15 _____- focused coping

16 _____-focused coping

Flash Cards

Name several rites of passage that occur in Western societies.	Why are adolescent girls briefly taller than adolescent boys?
Which hormones trigger the onset of puberty?	What caused the secular trends associated with puberty?
How have girls' view of menstruation changed over the past decade or so?	Why are girls apt to be even less pleased with the changes their bodies are undergoing during puberty than boys?
Why is early maturation both a plus and a minus to boys?	Why is it harder for American girls who are early maturers than for German girls who are early maturers?
Why is adolescent obesity even more troubling than childhood obesity?	Do anorexics avoid food?

Because they begin their growth spurt about two years earlier

Bar and bat mitzvah, confirmations, graduations

Increased health and nutrition

Estrogens (the female hormones) and androgens (the male hormones)

Girls' bodies typically become fatter at puberty, and this is in opposition to society's emphasis upon slenderness

Girls feel more positive about menstruation, and reaching menarche raises their self-esteem.

Our society is more ambivalent about sexuality, and so signs of sexual maturation are met with less approval.

It's a plus because they are larger than other boys and hence good at sports; it's bad because they spend time with older boys.

No, they often read cookbooks and cook for others. They merely do not themselves eat.

Health risks become more likely and adolescents are more self-conscious about their bodies.

Which girls are most likely
to become bulimic?

Describe the families of girls
with eating disorders.

What is the best way to treat
eating disorders?

What happens immediately in the
body when one encounters
a threat?

What is the difference between
primary and secondary appraisal?

Use four adjectives to
characterize the worst stressors.

According to Marx et. al., what are
some of the worst stressors?

Give an example of
problem-focused coping.

Give an example of
emotion-focused coping.

Give an example of
defensive coping.

Name some of the most commonly
used relaxation techniques.

Why did drug use decline
in the early 1980s?

The parents are frequently overly-demanding or there are other family problems.	Early physical maturers and those who were depressed as children
The sympathetic nervous system turns on, causing increased respiration, increased heart rate, and sweating.	A combination of dietary modification and psychotherapy works best.
They are *uncontrollable, unpredictable, simultaneous negative* events	In primary appraisal you evaluate the stressor; in secondary appraisal, you evaluate yourself.
Talking to your neighbor whose stereo is keeping you up all night.	Death of a spouse, getting married, death of a close family member, divorce, marital separation, death of a friend.
Telling yourself that it really isn't important if you get thrown out of a school	Telling yourself that no matter how bad you feel now, the situation will be resolved by next week
A lot of resources were invested in "Just Say No" campaigns.	Yoga, hypnosis, progressive muscle relaxation, meditation.

Name several illegal drugs whose use has risen in the 1990s.

List five reasons that adolescents use illegal drugs.

How are non-binge drinkers affected by binge drinkers?

What happens when someone becomes biologically addicted to a drug?

Name several techniques used by the National Public Service Research Board to curtail adolescent drug use.

List, in order, the three most common causes of adolescent death.

Why don't teens practice safe sex?

What suggestions does the text give about minimizing one's risk of contracting AIDs?

Name two STDs more common among teenagers than among older adults.

Pleasure; stress relief; thrill; influence of role-models; peer pressure

Marijuana, cocaine, crack, stimulants, heroin, and hallucinogenic drugs

The person needs ever-larger quantities of that drug if it is to have an effect on them.

Their sleep is disturbed by them, they are insulted by them, and they may be the target of unwelcome sexual advances.

Accidents, homicide, suicide

They provide alternative pastimes and mentoring, they educate teens as to drugs' dangers, and they try to prevent local cigarette advertising.

Use condoms; avoid high-risk behaviors such as anal intercourse; know your partner's sexual history; practice abstinence.

Because they feel invulnerable and at low risk for catching an STD

Chlamydia and gonorrhea

Practice Test One

1. Girls tend to hit puberty
   a. 2 years earlier than boys.
   b. about the same time as boys.
   c. 1 year after boys.
   d. 2 years after boys.

2. Which is the least common adolescent response to the physical changes associated with puberty?
   a. indifference
   b. embarrassment
   c. horror
   d. joy

3. Which teen most likely had the most difficult time during adolescence?
   a. Stan, an early-maturing boy
   b. Krista, an early-maturing girl
   c. Phillip, a late-maturing boy
   d. Darlene, a late-maturing girl

4. Barbara is a 15-year old girl who has recently lost control of her eating behavior. Even though it makes her feel guilty, several times a week she sneaks into her room and eats an entire box of cookies. She then makes herself throw up. Barbara most likely suffers from
   a. obesity.
   b. anorexia nervosa.
   c. bulimia.
   d. manic-depression.

5. Amalia has just learned that her car needs several thousands of dollars worth of repairs. She has spent the last half hour looking at her checkbook, calling her mother and asking for a loan, and juggling her budget. She has decided she can get the repairs done. Amalia has been
   a. engaged in primary evaluation.
   b. engaged in secondary evaluation.
   c. seeking social support.
   d. both [b] and [c]

6. Which of the following would likely make a stress worse?
   a. having only that one particular stress to concentrate on
   b. getting all the details about a situation so that it becomes clearer
   c. having the situation taken out of your own direct control
   d. being told that the outcome has no real effect on your status

7. Which of the following can be caused by stress?
   a. skin rashes
   b. back aches
   c. the common cold
   d. all of the above

8. Moses is in the middle of a crisis: he fears he might be developing AIDS. Which of the following should he avoid?
   a. problem-focused coping
   b. defensive coping
   c. seeking social support
   d. emotion-focused coping

9. Changing the definition of a situation
    a. can be beneficial if it is not too distorted.
    b. is never of use: reality is reality.
    c. involves enlisting social support.
    d. none of the above are true

10. Which of the following statements is true?
    a. Drug use is lower now than at any time in the past 25 years.
    b. Marijuana use has recently risen, but use of most other illegal drugs is down.
    c. Drug use is higher now than at any time in the past 25 years.
    d. Drug use is higher now than in the late 1980s, but lower than in the 1970s.

11. Sabra has been using cocaine for the past several months and has developed a psychological addition to it. Which of the following is true?
    a. Her body has changed so that it needs the drug to function.
    b. She can easily stop taking the drug if she so chooses.
    c. She feels that she cannot function or cope without using cocaine.
    d. All of the above

12. Roy is a regular binge drinker. That means he drinks
    a. more than 5 drinks at a sitting.   c. more than 15 times per month.
    b. more than 5 times per week.   d. more than 10 drinks at a sitting.

13. Sixteen-year old Roberto occasionally smokes. He probably has had no more than 15 cigarettes since he took his first puff at 12. Roberto will most likely
    a. stop smoking altogether.
    b. continue to smoke infrequently.
    c. increase his usage but remain an occasional smoker.
    d. become an addicted, habitual smoker.

14. The three most common causes of adolescent death, in decreasing order of frequency are
    a. natural causes, accidents, and suicide.   c. accidents, natural causes, and suicide.
    b. accidents, homicide, and suicide.   d. suicide, accidents, and natural causes.

15. The most common sexually transmitted disease is
    a. chlamydia.   c. genital herpes.
    b. AIDs.   d. gonorrhea.

16. Fifteen-year-old Ronnie seems to have changed during the past 8 months. His grades have dropped from As to Bs and Cs, he has begun telling lies, and he gets angry easily. In addition, he has dropped off the school's track team and he seems lost in his own world. Which of the following would you suspect?
    a. that Ronnie is contemplating suicide
    b. that Ronnie is severely depressed
    c. that Ronnie has been abusing drugs
    d. that Ronnie is experiencing normal adolescent anxiety and "growing pains"

Test Solutions

Self-Quiz Solution

1. a (page 416)
2. a (page 418)
3. c (page 420)
4. c (page 422)
5. d (page 224)
6. c (page 425)
7. d (page 425)
8. b (page 427)

9. a (page 427)
10. d (page 430)
11. c (page 431)
12. a (page 431)
13. d (page 434)
14. b (page 435)
15. a (page 438)
16. c (page 439

Crossword Puzzle Solution

CHAPTER 14

Cognitive Development in Adolescence

INTERESTING AND IMPORTANT THINGS YOU'LL KNOW AFTER READING THIS CHAPTER...

1. Why are adolescents so much smarter than children? See page 446.

2. What makes many adolescents so self-centered and critical? See page 449.

3. How do men's and women's moral reasoning differ? See page 453.

4. Who does well in high school, and who does not? See pages 455 and 456.

5. How common is it to graduate from college? See page 460.

6. Which career might best fit your personality? See page 467.

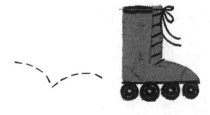

Intellectual Development

Piagetian approaches to cognitive development: Using formal operations

Information-processing perspectives: Gradual transformations in abilities

Egocentrism in thinking: Adolescents' self-absorption

Moral Development

Kohlberg's theory of moral development: Describing moral reasoning

Gilligan's theory of moral development: Focusing on girls

School Performance and Moral Development

Socioeconomic status and school performance: Individual differences in achievement

Ethnicity and school achievement

Are there psychological costs to academic achievement? It depends on your culture

College: Pursuing higher education

The demographics of higher education

Gender and college performance

Overcoming gender and racial barriers to achievement

Picking an Occupation: Choosing Life's Work

Ginzberg's career choice theory

Holland's personality type theory

Gender and career choice: Women's work

Choosing a career

Learning Objectives

When you have mastered the material in this chapter, you should be able to ...

1. Describe the cognitive advances that occur once an individual attains formal operations. (page 446)

2. Discuss the weaknesses as well as the strengths of Piaget's views of cognitive development. (page 447)

3. Present the information processors' perspective on cognitive development during adolescence. (page 448)

4. Describe the manifestations and consequences of adolescent egocentrism. (page 449)

5. Outline Kohlberg's theory of moral development. (page 451)

6. Summarize Gilligan's theory of moral development. (453)

7. Describe the relationship between socioeconomic status and school performance and understand the reason for that relationship. (page 455)

8. Describe the relationship between ethnicity and school performance and understand the reason for that relationship. (page 456)

9. Understand the cultural variation between pressure to succeed academically and feelings of stress. (page 458)

10. Discuss the demographics of college attendance and college graduation. (page 460)

11. Describe how one's gender influences one's college experience. (page 461)

12. Provide one suggestion as to how to decrease both gender and ethnic differences in academic achievement. (page 464)

13. Relate Ginsberg's career choice theory. (page 465)

14. Describe Holland's personality types and know what careers best suit them. (page 466)

15. Contrast communal and agentic professions and understand some of the remaining gender inequities in the workplace. (page 468)

16. Describe several guidelines for selecting a career. (page 469)

Guided Review

Intellectual Development

Piaget's _____ and final stage of cognitive development is termed the _____ operational stage. In this stage, usually beginning at about age _____, adolescents can use _____ to solve _____ problems. Their problem-solving becomes _____ and they now use _____-deductive reasoning. Although Piaget claimed that it was not until _____ that adolescents mastered formal operations entirely, we now know that a _____ percentage of American adults never attain it fully. Furthermore, formal operational logic is _____ in all cultures.

fourth (446)
formal (446)
12 (446); logic (446)
abstract (446)
systematic (446); hypothetico (446) 15 (447)

large (447)

not valued (447)

Recent research has pointed to a number of weaknesses in Piaget's original formulation of cognitive development. In particular, cognitive development is not as globally _____ as he imagined, and children's performance is more _____ than he claimed. Many developmentalists have rejected a _____-approach to cognitive development, and see intellectual growth as more _____. In general, Piaget _____ children's abilities, and he had a _____ perspective about what constitutes "thinking."

consistent (447)
uneven (447)

stage (447)
gradual (447); underestimated (447); narrow (447)

Information processors attribute the cognitive growth seen in adolescence to changes in the ways that information is _____, to use of better _____, and to increases in _____ and selective _____. They concur with Piaget that adolescents master the ability to think _____ and _____. As their _____ stores increase, so do their problem-solving abilities. _____, the knowledge that people have of their own thinking processes, improves greatly. IQ, however, remains _____.

organized (448) strategies (448); memory (448); attention (448); abstractly (448) hypothetically (448); knowledge (448); Metacognition (448)
stable (448)

With these increased cognitive skills comes a period of adolescent _____. During this period, adolescents are _____ of others and self-_____. Adolescents develop what _____ has termed the "imaginary _____"; in other words, they act as if they are the center of everyone's attention. This belief usually leads to self-_____. A second distortion caused by egocentrism is the personal _____, the erroneous belief that one is special and unique. When caught up in this belief, adolescents feel that no one can _____ them and they also feel _____. This leads to _____ behavior

egocentrism (449); critical (449); absorbed (449)
Elkind (449); audience (449)

consciousness (449)
fable (449)

understand (449)
invulnerable (449); risk-taking (449)

Moral Development

Kohlberg (451)
stages (451); cognitive (451)

three (451)
two (451); Preconventional
(451); rewards (451)
punishments (451); conventional (451); good (451)
society (451)
1/4 (451); universal (451)

laws (451)
postconventional (451)

behavior (451)

According to Lawrence _____, individuals pass through a series of _____ of moral development as their _____ abilities become more sophisticated. His scheme breaks moral development into _____ major levels, each of which has _____ substages. _____ moral reasoning, the lowest level, involves moral reasoning based upon _____ and _____. In the second level, _____ moral reasoning, morality is based upon one's desire to be seen as a _____ person or member of _____. The final stage — which is attained by about _____ of adults — involves using _____ moral principles that are seen as more important than the _____ of any particular society. This last stage is called _____ moral reasoning. One problem with Kohlberg's theory is that moral reasoning does not always translate into moral _____.

male (453)
girls' (453)
Gilligan (453)
justice (453)
compassion (453)
3 (453)

survival (453)

sacrifice (453); always (453)

nonviolence (453)
themselves (453); anyone else
(453)
large (453)

A second problem with Kohlberg's theory is that it is based almost entirely upon data collected from _____ subjects. Some psychologists argue that it does not reflect _____ moral development. According to Carol _____, boys are taught to be more concerned with _____, while girls are taught to be more concerned with _____. Gilligan, there- fore, has proposed an alternative _____-stage sequence of female moral development. During the first stage, the ori- entation towards individual _____, girls think selfishly. During the second stage, termed "goodness as self- _____," females believe that they should _____ put others' needs ahead of their own. In the final stage, "the morality of _____," women come to realize that hurting _____ is as immoral as hurting _____.

At this point in time, it is unclear exactly how _____ gender differences in moral reasoning really are.

School Performance and Cognitive Development

decline (455)
difficult (455)

harshly (455)

Somewhat surprisingly, students' grades _____ as they get older. This is in part due to the more _____ nature of the material and because teachers grade older students more _____.

Socioeconomic differences in school achievement are _____ during adolescence than during childhood. Adolescents raised in poverty often suffer from poorer _____, live in _____ conditions, and lack scholastic _____. These adolescents' parents are _____ likely to be involved in their schooling, and the schools these teens attend are often _____ and have high levels of _____.

greater (455)

health (455); crowded (455)
resources (455); less (455)

inadequate (455); violence (455)

Although almost no developmentalist believes that these lower achievements are _____ based, that argument was made in the book, *The Bell* _____. One reason to reject this argument is the wider variation in school achievement _____ each socioeconomic class as compared to _____ socioeconomic classes. It is not surprising that the gap between rich and poor teens widens with age, since being able to master one year's academic material depends upon having mastered the _____ year's. Thus, a _____ situation of failure is set up.

genetically (455)
Curve (455)

within (456); between (456)

previous (456); snowballing (456)

_____, too, plays a role in school success. In particular, _____ and _____ teens get lower grades than Caucasian teens, while _____ teens get higher grades. The _____ pattern is identical. In part these ethnic differences are caused by differences in _____ status; when income is held constant, the differences become _____. In addition, it appears that members of some minority groups believe that _____ will prevent them from succeeding no matter how hard they try, and so they are _____ to try. Immigrants who come to a country _____ are more likely to do well in school than immigrants whose entrance was _____. _____ about the causes of school success are also a factor, with those students who believe that _____ leads to success more willing to work _____ than students who do not. Finally, _____ has argued that African-American and _____ students tend to believe that they can succeed _____ poor school performance; Asian-American students tend to believe that they _____ be successful if they've done poorly in school. Again, these beliefs influence a student's _____ to put effort into academics.

Ethnicity (456)
African-American (456); Hispanic (456); Asian-American (456); dropout (457)
socioeconomic (457)
much smaller (457)

prejudice (457)
unwilling (457)
voluntarily (457)

forced (457); Attributions (457)

effort (458); hard (458)
Steinberg (458)
Hispanic (458)
despite (458)
cannot (458)

willingness (458)

Cram (458)

pressure (458)

less (459)

competing (459)
social (459); employment (459)
secondary (459)
conflict (459); time (459)

1/2 (460)
1/3 (460)

declined (460)
financial aid (460)
40% (460)
30% (461)
ethnic (461)

greater (461)

half (461)
social (461)
mathematics (461); physical (461)
drop out (461); Caucasian (461); minority (461); gender (461); earn (462)

above (462)

differently (462)
eye contact (462); call (462)
time (462);
positive (462)
single-sex (462)

science (462)
attention (462); encouragement (463); role models (463)

_____ schools are common-place in parts of Asia, and immigrants from these areas are starting these schools in the U.S. These schools are indicative of the _____ that is placed upon some Asian and Asian-American students to do well academically. Surprisingly, a recent study shows that Asian students experience _____ stress than American students in spite of the pressure they are under. The reason appears to be that American students are more stressed because there are so many _____ demands on them: school, _____ pursuits, part-time _____. Asian students, in contrast, feel other demands are _____ and experience less _____ over how to spend their _____.

Fewer than _____ of Caucasian high school graduates and fewer than _____ of African-American and Hispanic high school graduates enter college. The proportion of the minority population that enters college has _____ over the past decade, largely due to cut-backs in _____. Only about _____ of those who enroll in college graduate in four years, and another _____ finish their degrees at some point. Again, the _____ differences in graduation rates mimic those of entrance rates. The make-up of college student bodies will continue to change, however, as minority youth make up a _____ percentage of the 18-year-old population.

Although women make up roughly _____ of the college population, they are over-represented in _____ science classes and under-represented in _____ and the _____ sciences. If women do enroll in these courses, they are more likely to _____. This is true for both _____ and _____ women. This reflects our history of _____ bias. College men expect to _____ more than women after they graduate, and they are more likely to see themselves as _____ average in ability.

Even though most are unaware of it, professors treat male and female students _____. In particular, they make more _____ with male students, _____ on them more frequently, give them more _____ outside of class, and give them more _____ feedback. These facts have caused some to argue in favor of _____ colleges for women. Women who attend these colleges do more often go into _____. Women students who attend single-sex colleges receive more _____ and _____ from professors and are exposed to more female _____.

One interesting study demonstrated that women's success depends upon their _____ of success. In particular, when women were given a test which had been described as more difficult for women than for men, they performed _____ than the men; when told there were no gender differences, they performed _____ as the men. This study demonstrates the way that _____ and _____ stereotypes can influence academic success.

expectation (464)

more poorly (464)

as well (464)
gender (464); ethnic (464)

Picking an Occupation: Choosing Life's Work

Eli _____ has proposed a _____-stage model of career selection. During childhood one is in the _____ stage of career development, and focuses on careers without a thought to one's _____. People become more practical during the _____ stage, which spans _____, and integrate their _____ and values into their decisions. Finally, in early _____, people enter the _____ stage, and explore career options through _____ and actual _____. Several problems exist with Ginsberg's theory. First, it assumes that people believe that they have _____ (not necessarily true for _____ individuals). Second, his age ranges are too _____.

Ginsberg (465); 3 (465)
fantasy (465)

abilities (465)
tentative (465); adolescence (465); goals (465)
adulthood (465); realistic (465); education (465)
experience (465)
options (466)
lower-class (466)
rigid (466)

John _____ theory emphasizes the role of _____ in career satisfaction. _____ persons are practical but lack _____ skills; according to Holland, they make good _____ and _____. _____ like the theoretical; they excel in careers involving _____ and _____. "Social" individuals are very _____ and so make fine _____ and _____. "Conventional" individuals like _____; they succeed best as _____ or bank _____. _____ individuals thrive on _____ and are good leaders. Therefore, according to Holland, _____ is the right choice for them. Finally, _____ individuals like to use art to _____ themselves and so do well in those occupations that involve art. The main problem with Holland's theory is that not everyone fits neatly into just _____ personality type.

Holland's (466); personality (466); Realistic (466); social (466); farmers (466)
laborers (466); Intellectuals (467); math (467); science (467); verbal (467); teachers (467); salespersons (467); Structure (467); secretaries (467); tellers (467); Enterprising (467); risk (467); management (467); artistic (467); express (467);

one (467)

Traditionally, _____ were considered best suited for jobs involving helping others, the so-called _____ professions. Men, in contrast, were channeled towards the _____ professions, which consist of jobs in which something tangible is _____. Communal professions usually have _____ prestige and _____ than agentic professions.

women (468)
communal (468)
agentic (468)

produced (468)
lower (468); wages (468)

decreased (468)
less (468);
more (468);
Most (568);
almost all (468)

within (468)

glass (468)

variety (469)
strengths (469); weaknesses
(469); pros (469); cons (469);
internships (470)

Although job discrimination has _____, it still does exist. For example, on average, women earn _____ than men in identical jobs. Still, _____ women are working outside the home than in the past. _____ American adult women work for wages, and _____ will work outside the home at some point in their lives. Although many new careers have opened up for women, discrimination still exists _____ those careers. Women and members of minority groups frequently encounter the _____ ceiling, the invisible barrier above which they cannot rise.

Adolescents considering their career options would be well-advised to consider a _____ of jobs before choosing one. They should be realistic about their _____ and _____. Keep notes about the _____ and _____ of each career possibility. Finally, participate in _____ to get on the job experience.

Crossword Puzzle

Cognitive Development in Adolescence

Across

1 The first stage of career development

3 Traditionally, women were relegated to these professions.

6 These Holland types feel the need to creatively express themselves.

9 _____ moral reasoning is based upon moral principles.

14 Hypothetico-_____ reasoning

15 Carol _____ is one of Kohlberg's strongest critics.

16 The imaginary _____ consists of fictitious observers.

17 The orientation toward individual _____, Gilligan's first stage

18 The _____ ceiling keeps women and minorities from being promoted past a certain level of management.

20 A state of self-absorption

21 Lawrence _____ developed the most influential theory of moral development.

22 _____ operations, Piaget is final stage of cognitive development

Down

2 Traditionally, only men were channeled into these careers.

4 The knowledge people have about their own thinking processes

5 Personal _____ makes adolescents feel unique and exceptional.

7 The stage in career development in which people explore possible career options

8 _____ moral reasoning is based upon the need for others' approval.

9 _____ moral reasoning is based on expected rewards and punishments.

10 The orientation of self-_____, Gilligan's second moral stage

11 The morality of _____, Gilligan's most advanced moral stage

12 These Holland types make good managers or politicians.

13 The stage of career development that occurs during adolescence

19 These Holland types make good salespersons and teachers.

Flash Cards

Describe one of the tests Piaget used to determine whether an adolescent had reached formal operations.

If you could use three words to describe formal operational thought, what would they be?

Describe the kinds of cultures most likely to produce citizens who use formal operational thought.

List five criticisms of Piaget's theory.

What good has come from Piaget's work?

Give an example of how metacognition can help one succeed.

How does adolescent egocentrism change adolescents?

Why is adolescent egocentrism harmful?

Contrast the two levels of preconventional moral reasoning.

Contrast the two levels of conventional moral reasoning.

Abstract, hypothetical, and systematic	He asked them to determine what influences the speed at which a pendulum swings. The key is to systematically hold all factors but one consistent.
Not universal; children are inconsistent; change is gradual; his definition of thinking is narrow; he underestimated children	Technologically sophisticated societies that have formal education.
It can help you estimate how long you will need to study in order to fully master the test material.	He spurred a tremendous number of studies and stimulated much classroom reform.
The personal fable encourages risky behavior and makes adolescents feel misunderstood.	It makes them more critical of others, and less open to criticism of themselves. It makes them more self-conscious and makes them feel invulnerable.
In stage 3, individuals want others to respect and like them; in stage 4, individuals want to conform to society's rules.	In stage 1 individuals act to avoid punishment; in stage 2, they act to maximize reward.

Contrast the two levels of postconventional moral reasoning.

Describe the data concerning the relationship between moral reasoning and moral behavior.

Name Kohlberg's stages of moral development.

Name Gilligan's stages of moral development.

What are the two main complaints against Kohlberg's theory?

According to Gilligan, what is the essence of the gender difference in moral reasoning?

Why do high-schoolers receive lower grades than elementary- and middle-schoolers?

List five environmental contributors to the fact that poor adolescents do worse in school than middle-class adolescents.

Summarize the argument presented in *The Bell Curve*.

Give a piece of evidence countering a genetic explanation of the relationship between poverty and poor school performance.

Why is the gap between rich and poor adolescents' school performance greater than the gap between rich and poor children's?

List five reasons for ethnic differences in school achievement.

It is mixed. Sometimes moral reasoning appears to influence moral behavior, but the relationship is not always strong.	In stage 5, individuals act to uphold society's principles; in stage 6, individuals act on their individual consciousness.
Orientation towards individual survival; goodness as self-sacrifice; morality of nonviolence	Preconventional, conventional, postconventional
Men are more concerned with justice; women are more concerned with compassion.	(1) Moral reasoning is not always closely tied to moral behavior. (2) His theory is based largely upon data from male subjects.
(1) Worse health; (2) more crowded, chaotic homes; (3) fewer academic resources; (4) parents less involved; (5) worse schools	The material is more difficult and the teachers grade them more strictly.
There is more within SES group variation in school achievement than there is between group variation.	The poor are genetically less well-endowed than the wealthy. They are poor *because* they have low IQs and so get low-paying jobs. Their children also have low IQs.
(1) SES; (2) beliefs that prejudice will prevent success; (3) forced immigration; (4) belief in relation between work and success; (5) lack of perceived need for grades	Poor school performance tends to steadily worsen, since negative self-fulfilling prophecies are set up and since it is hard to catch up on what has already been missed.

Why do American adolescents feel more stress than Asian adolescents in spite of less parental pressure?

What percentage of American high school graduates graduate from college?

What kinds of college classes do women take and not take?

What are the benefits of single-sex colleges for women?

List the three stages of Ginsberg's theory of career development in the correct sequence.

Why does Ginsberg's theory fail to work well for underprivileged individuals?

List Holland's six personality types.

Give several examples of communal professions.

Give several examples of agentic professions.

Why has the pay differential between men and women decreased?

28%: 40% enroll, and 40% of those (16%) graduate in 4 years while 30% of the others (12%) take longer.	Asian adolescents feel that their only serious goal is to get good grades; Americans feel pressure to do well in school, to be popular, and to work part-time.
Women receive more attention and encouragement from professors, are less likely to avoid science classes, and have more female role-models.	They tend to take social science and education classes, and not to take mathematics, engineering, and physical science classes.
Children raised in poverty don't fantasize about possible careers and they do not take as long to choose one because they feel that their options are limited.	(1) Fantasy, until age 11; (2) tentative, adolescence; (3) realistic, young adulthood
Teaching, nursing, counseling, being a librarian	Artistic; enterprising; intellectual; social; realistic; conventional
Not because women are earning more money, but due to the loss of high-paying manufacturing jobs for men.	Construction work, architecture, being a chef, novelist

Practice Test One

1. Thirteen-year-old Wesley has entered the stage of formal operations. Which of the following is most likely *false*?
   a. He has just begun to think abstractly.
   b. He has just begun to think hypothetically.
   c. He has just begun to think systematically.
   d. He has just begun to solve transitive inference problems.

2. Piaget was most correct about
   a. the broad picture of cognitive development.
   b. the timing of cognitive development.
   c. the pace of cognitive development.
   d. the universality of cognitive development.

3. Which of the following does *not* increase during adolescence?
   a. IQ
   b. memory
   c. metacognition
   d. the ability to divide one's attention

4. Last night, Nadia wrote the following in her diary: "No one understands how I feel, not even my friends." Nadia is experiencing
   a. hypothetico-deductive reasoning.
   b. metacognitive awareness.
   c. a personal fable.
   d. an imaginary audience.

5. Lucia says: "I returned the wallet I found because I wanted to make my parents proud of me. They would have been ashamed if I had kept it." Lucia is
   a. a preconventional moral reasoner.
   b. a conventional moral reasoner.
   c. a postconventional moral reasoner.
   d. orienting to individual survival.

6. Mala says: "He asked me to prepare his inventory for him. I had to say 'no'. I would've done it if I could, but I'm really swamped with my own work and I've got tons of deadlines coming up. So I told him I'd help him for an hour." Mala is
   a. atypical .
   b. at Gilligan's highest level of moral reasoning.
   c. at Gilligan's middle level of moral reasoning.
   d. orienting to individual survival.

7. Which of the following is least likely to be a cause of socioeconomic differences in school performance?
   a. the fact that poverty-class students have fewer educational resources available to them
   b. the fact that poverty-class students are less bright due to genetic factors
   c. the fact that middle-class students have parents who are more involved in their education
   d. the fact that middle-class students usually have a quiet, private place to study

8. Which of the following groups of students tend to get the best grades in school?
   a. African-American students
   b. Asian-American students
   c. Caucasian students
   d. Hispanic students

9. _____ students as a group feel very stressed because _____.
   a. Asian; they are pressured to do well in school
   b. Asian; they feel many competing pressures
   c. American; they are pressured to do well in school
   d. American; they feel many competing pressures

10. How has minority-student college attendance changed during the past decade?
    a. An increasing proportion of minority students now attends college since discrimination has decreased.
    b. An increasing proportion of minority students now attends college since inner-city schools have improved.
    c. A decreasing proportion of minority students now attends college since fewer minority students now desire to attend.
    d. A decreasing proportion of minority students now attends college since financial aid is less available.

11. Which of the following *does not* contribute to the fact that female college students do more poorly in physical science classes than male students?
    a. They receive less positive feedback from their professors.
    b. They have been taught that women do poorly in these classes.
    c. They receive less help outside the classroom from their professors.
    d. They do not study as hard because they believe that they do not need to.

12. Which, according to Steele and Aronson, would be the best way to equalize gender and ethnic academic achievement?
    a. Decrease stereotypes as to who can do well.
    b. Target increases in school funding to those who are not doing well.
    c. Change teachers' and professors' behaviors .
    d. Devise both peer and adult mentoring programs.

13. Imelda has recently decided that she wants to become a missionary when she grows up because she feels that it is important to spread the word of God and help people in need. Imelda is most likely
    a. about 6 years old.
    b. about 8 years old.
    c. about 10 years old.
    d. about 12 years old.

14. Adam just received the results of a career counseling test that he took last week, and the report says that he has a "conventional" personality. According to Holland, which career would best suit him?
    a. being an artist
    b. being a teacher
    c. being a secretary
    d. being a manager

15. Which of the following statements is true?
    a. Women usually earn the same amount of money as men if they do the same work.
    b. Women are just as likely to be promoted to top management as men, if they do a good job.
    c. Young adults who are engineers and doctors are just as likely to be women as to be men.
    d. Almost all American women work at some point during their lifetimes.

16. In general, people should
    a. sample broadly before settling upon a career.
    b. select a career and then stick to it.
    c. chose a career that matches their interests, even if it doesn't match their abilities.
    d. all of the above

Test Solutions

Self-Quiz Solution

1. d (page 446)
2. a (page 447)
3. a (page 448)
4. c (page 449)
5. b (page 451)
6. b (page 453)
7. b (page 455)
8. b (page 456)

9. d (page 458)
10. d (page 460)
11. d (page 462)
12. a (page 464)
13. d (page 465)
14. c (page 437)
15. d (page 468)
16. a (page 469

Crossword Puzzle Solution

CHAPTER 15

Social and Personality Development in Adolescence

INTERESTING AND IMPORTANT THINGS YOU'LL KNOW AFTER READING THIS CHAPTER...

1. What are the signs that someone is planning suicide, and how can you try to prevent him or her? See page 484.

2. How big is the "generation gap;" how different are adolescents' and parents' values? See page 487.

3. How large a problem is juvenile delinquency? See page 495.

4. At what age do most American adolescents begin engaging in sexual intercourse? See page 498.

5. What determines whether a person is straight or gay? See page 500.

6. Which sex education programs work? See page 503.

IDENTITY: ASKING "WHO AM I?"

Self-concept: Characterizing the characteristics of adolescence

Self-esteem: Evaluating oneself

Identity formation in adolescence: Change or crisis?

Marcia's approach to identity formation: Updating Erikson

Depression and suicide: Psychological difficulties in adolescence

Deterring adolescent suicide

RELATIONSHIPS: FAMILY AND FRIENDS

Family ties: Reassessing relations with relations

Relationships with peers: The importance of belonging

Race segregation: The great divide of adolescence

Popularity and rejection: Adolescent likes and dislikes

Conformity: Peer pressure in adolescence

Juvenile delinquency: The crimes of adolescence

DATING, SEXUAL BEHAVIOR, AND TEENAGE PREGNANCY

Dating: Boy meets girl in the 1990s

Sexual relationships: Permissiveness with affection

Sexual orientation: Heterosexuality and homosexuality

Teenage pregnancy: A problem of epidemic proportions

Preventing adolescent pregnancies: Sex education programs that work

Learning Objectives

When you have mastered the material in this chapter, you should be able to ...

1. Describe how adolescents' self-concepts are different from children's. (page 477)

2. Discuss the influences on adolescents' feelings of self-esteem. (page 477)

3. Characterize the identity search, and know the differences between Marcia's four identity statuses. (page 478)

4. Describe the prevalence of adolescent depression, and know which adolescents are most at risk for becoming depressed. (page 481)

5. Explain how the adolescent suicide rate has changed over the past few decades and know who is most likely to attempt or commit suicide. (page 482)

6. Relate the steps that should be taken if you suspect that someone is contemplating suicide. (page 484)

7. Discuss how increasing adolescent autonomy changes relationships within the family, and describe when and about what most disagreements occur. (page 487)

8. Explain why peers and peer approval is so important to adolescents. (page 489)

9. Contrast cliques and crowds, and be able to identify some of the more common crowds. (page 490)

10. Explain how cross-sex interaction evolves during adolescence and how this affects peer group structure. (page 491)

11. Provide explanations for the voluntary racial segregation that occurs in many high schools and college. (page 492)

12. Characterize popular, controversial, neglected, and rejected adolescents. (page 493)

13. Describe how conformity changes from childhood to adulthood, and be able to describe the situations in which adolescents are most likely to bow to peer pressure. (page 494)

14. Describe the magnitude of America's juvenile delinquency problem, and be able to contrast socialized and undersocialized delinquents. (page 495)

15. Discuss the prevalence of and functions of dating. (page 497)

16. Describe adolescents' attitudes about and practice of masturbation. (page 498)

17. Present the most common adolescent attitude about sexual intercourse and know at what age this behavior is likely to begin. (page 498)

18. Discuss the factors that influence sexual orientation. (page 499)

19. Explain the magnitude and consequences of America's teenage pregnancy epidemic. (page 500)

20. Enumerate the characteristics of effective sex education programs. (page 502)

Guided Review

Identity: Asking "Who Am I?"

Adolescence is a time of pondering one's _____. _____ changes, especially the ability to think _____, and _____ changes, especially those involving sexual maturation, bring the issue of identity to the foreground.

identity (476); Cognitive (476)
abstractly (476)
physical (476)

Adolescents' self-concepts, and hence their self-_____ are more sophisticated than those made by children. They know how _____ see them and know that their friends views are not always _____. Their self-concepts become more _____ and they can examine different aspects of themselves _____. Early adolescents are sometimes troubled by the _____ that they see in themselves.

descriptions (477)

others (477)
accurate (477)
coherent (477)
simultaneously (477)
inconsistencies (477)

As self-concept becomes more differentiated, so does self-_____. Girls tend to have _____ self-esteem than boys, especially during _____ adolescence. This is because girls are more concerned about their _____ and _____ status. In addition, many girls feel in a double bind because they believe that _____ success may lead to a decrease in _____. _____ level also effects self-esteem. Wealthier adolescents tend to have _____ self-esteem than poorer adolescents, especially in _____ and _____ adolescence. Nowadays, ethnicity contributes _____ to self-esteem levels.

esteem (477); lower (477)
early (477)
appearance (478); social (478)

academic (478)
popularity (478);
Socioeconomic (478); higher (478) middle (478); late (478)
little (478)

Ethnicity and gender interact to form _____ effects on self-esteem; for example, _____ and _____ males often have particularly high self-esteem levels.

ethgender (478)
African-American (478);
Hispanic (478)

Erikson proposed that during adolescence individuals experience the identity-versus-identity _____ stage of psychosocial development and feel driven to _____ themselves. They are presented with many _____ and must make important _____ for themselves. Adolescents rely on their _____ to help them find their identities.

confusion (479)
understand (479)
choices (479)
decisions (479)
peers (479)

Marcia 480)
four (480)

crisis (480)
chooses (480)
commitment (480); investment
(480)
achieved (480); adjusted (480)
achievement (480)
foreclosures (480)
others (480)
rigid (480)
approval (480); authoritarian
(480); diffusions (480);
shift (480)
relationships (480); moratori-
ums (481)
anxious (481)
identity (481)

Most (481)
20-35 (481); 25-40 (481)

3 (481)
major (481); more (482)
inwards (482)
externalize (482)
aggressive (482); drugs (482);
African-American (482);
genetic (482)
environment (482)
death (482); rejection (482)

third (483)
tripled (483)
90 minutes (483)
underestimate (483); more
(483); less (483)
violent (483)
200 (483)
stress (483); depression (483)
abuse (483)
drug (483)
cluster (483)

James _____ expanded upon Erikson's work and proposed _____ different identity states. Which state one is in depends upon whether one has experienced an identity _____ — a period in which an adolescent consciously _____ among alternatives — and whether one has made an identity _____ — a psychological _____ in a course of action. Adolescents who have done both are called identity _____; they tend to be well-_____ and to have high _____ motivations. Individuals who made commitments without experiencing crises are called _____. These adolescents let _____ make their decisions for them. They are character- ized by _____ strength, which means they need others' _____ and are _____. Adolescents who have not experi- enced crises nor made commitments are called _____. These individuals frequently _____ their priorities and have trouble maintaining _____. Finally, _____ are those who have had crises but not yet settled upon commitments. These individuals often feel _____, but usually do find an _____ eventually. Individuals can move from one identity state to one of the others.

_____ adolescents have felt depressed at one time or anoth- er. In fact, about _____% of adolescent boys and _____% of adolescent girls report having felt depressed during the past six months. Still, only about ___% actually experience _____ depression. Girls are _____ likely to feel depressed than boys. This may be because they turn _____ when they experience stress; boys, in contrast, _____ the stress and become _____ or use _____. Some but not all studies sug- gest that _____ teens are more likely to feel depressed than Caucasian teens. Some individuals have a _____ predispo- sition to become depressed, but the _____ also plays a role. The _____ of a loved one or _____ can trigger depression.

Suicide, the _____ most common cause of death among adolescents, has _____ in the past 30 years. We know that one teenager commits suicide every _____ and that this number is an _____. Girls are _____ likely to attempt sui- cide than boys, but are _____ likely to succeed. This is because boys use more _____ means to kill themselves. There are about _____ attempts for every successful ado- lescent suicide. High levels of _____ and _____ increase an adolescent's risk, as does having a history of _____ and _____ use. Sometimes one suicide triggers others, so-called _____ suicides.

Warning signs that someone is considering suicide include: making suicidal _____, problems in _____, giving away _____ writing a _____, dramatic _____ change, and _____ with death.

statements (484); school (484)
possessions (484); will (484)
personality (484); preoccupation (484)

If you think that a friend is considering suicide, _____ to them, especially about their _____. If you feel that a suicide attempt is imminent, do not leave the person _____ and immediately seek _____ help. Remove any _____, and try to get a _____ from your friend that he will take no action until you've _____.

talk (485)
plans (485)

alone (485); professional (485)
weapons (485); promise (485)
spoken again (485)

Relationships: Family and Friends

As adolescents mature, they demand more _____ and want to have more _____ over their own lives. In many cases, this leads to some degree of _____ within the household. One reason this occurs is that adolescents come to see their parents in a less-_____ way. By late adolescence, power in the family is more _____ than it was previously, with _____ still exercising final control. American adolescents seek autonomy at relatively _____ ages.

autonomy (487)
control (487)
conflict (487)

idealized (487)
shared (487)
parents (487)
early (487)

Adolescents and their parents tend to have similar _____ and _____, and most adolescents _____ and _____ their parents. Most disagreements concern issues of _____. This conflict tends to peak during _____ adolescence; it wanes when parents begin to _____ more to their adolescents wishes. About _____ of families experience relatively little conflict overall.

attitudes (488)
values (488); love (488)
respect (488); personal choice (488); early (488)
yield (489)
80% (489)

As they get older, adolescents spend _____ amounts of time with their peers. Adolescents turn to peers for social _____ because peers _____ the same experiences. Peers provide _____ against which adolescents can measure their behavior. In addition, the quest for autonomy makes it less likely that adolescents would turn to their _____ for advice.

increasing (490)

comparison (490); share (490)
norms (490)

parents (490)

Adolescents usually belong to _____ different types of social groups. _____ are smaller — they have between _____ and _____ members — the members _____ interact. _____ are larger and are composed of individuals who share certain _____ but who _____ necessarily interact. Typical crowds include _____, _____, and _____.

two (490)
Cliques (490);
2 (490); 12 (490); frequently (490); Crowds (490)
characteristics (490); do not (490); toughs (490); jocks (490); populars (490)

same-sex (491)
cleavage (491); puberty (491)
cliques (491); dances (491)
both (491)
high-status (491)
declines (491)

male-female (491)

increases (492)

support (492)
is not (492)
socioeconomic (492); academic (492)
negative (493); majority (493)
minority (493); norms (493)

Popular (494)
controversial (494)
disliked (494)
many (494); disclose (494)
extracurricular (494); know (494); Neglected (494); reject-ed (494); disliked (494); less (494)
opposite (494)
lonely (494)

social (494)
expert (494)

increase (495)
change (495)

own (495); both (495)
declines (495)

At the beginning of adolescence, individuals spend almost all of their time in _____ groups. This is known as sex _____. After _____, boys' and girls' _____ begin to converge at _____ or parties. Soon new cliques, composed of _____ males and females, develop. These new cliques are initially composed of _____ individuals, but this changes over time. Clique influence _____ late in adolescence when individuals' efforts become primarily focused on _____ interactions.

Voluntary racial segregation _____ during adolescence. One reason this occurs is that minority students seek _____ from others who share their minority status. It may also be that race _____ what is causing the separation: _____ status and differences in _____ achievement may inadvertently contribute to racial segregation. Unfortunately, _____ attitudes among both _____ and _____ students also play a role, and clique _____ may prevent individuals from crossing racial lines.

_____ adolescents are those who are liked by almost everyone; _____ adolescents are liked by some and _____ by others. Teens of both types are apt to have _____ close friends, self-_____ to others, engage in _____ school activities, and _____ they are well-liked. _____ adolescents are ignored, while _____ adolescents are actively _____. These two types of teens are _____ likely to engage in social activities, spend less time with members of the _____ sex, and are more likely to feel _____.

Adolescents turn to their peers for advice in _____ matters because they consider those peers to be more _____ than their parents about those issues. Conformity doesn't really _____ during adolescence; it is more accurate to say that adolescents _____ to whom they are willing to conform. Eventually, as adults, most individuals will make their _____ decisions and conformity to _____ peer and parent pressures _____.

Adolescents commit a _____ high amount of crime, even of _____ crime and this trend is _____. _____ delinquents — the more dangerous type — have typically been raised by _____ parents and have failed to _____ appropriate self-control. These individuals were usually _____ children who were _____ by peers and who experienced _____ failure. As adults, many suffer from _____ personality disorder, and it is _____ that they will ever be successfully _____. In contrast, _____ delinquents are usually _____ motivated by peer pressure and they tend to engage in relatively _____ crimes. Most _____ breaking the law after they become adults.

disproportionately (495)
violent (495); increasing (495);
Undersocialized (495)
uncaring (495); learn (494)

aggressive (495); rejected (495); academic (495)
antisocial (495); unlikely (495)
rehabilitated (495); socialized (495); highly (495)
petty (495)
discontinue (495)

Dating, Sexual Behavior, and Teenage Pregnancy

By the time they are _____ or _____ most girls, and by the time they are _____ or _____, most boys have begun dating. Almost _____ have begun by _____, and by graduation about _____ will have been steadily involved with someone.

12 (497); 13 (497)
13 (497); 14 (497)
all (497); 16 (497)
3/4 (497)

Dating serves many functions. It is not only a form of _____, but it's also _____ and can affect one's _____. Little psychological _____ is shared among dating couples during _____ adolescence, but this changes during _____ adolescence. There is frequently conflict in _____ households, since the parents in these households may have had no experience with dating themselves.

courtship (497); fun (497); status (497); intimacy (497)
early and middle (497)
late (497)
immigrant (497)

Adolescence is the time of _____ awakening. Most adolescents' first sexual experiences involve _____. Boys begin at a(n) _____ age than girls, but the frequency with which they masturbate _____ during adolescence, whereas girls' frequency _____. Even though masturbation is _____, it often evokes _____ and _____. Some of this is due to negative _____ attitudes, and some is due to the erroneous belief that only _____ individuals masturbate.

sexual (498)
masturbation (498)
earlier (498)
declines (498)
increases (498)
common (498); guilt (498)
shame (498); historical (498)
undesirable (498)

half (498)
15 (498); 18 (498)
80% (498)
younger (498)

earlier (498)
ethnicity (498)
double (499)
males (499)
females (499)

affection (499)

heterosexual 499)

4% (500); 10% (500); homosexual (499); not rare (500)

continuum (500)

small (500)
genetic (500); hormonal (500)
environmental (500)
Freud's (500); learning (55)

choice (500)
no longer (500)
depression (500); suicide (500)

the same (500)

10 (500)
half (500)
negative (501)
drop out (501)
low-paying (501); welfare
(501); health (501)

children (501)
poor (501)
school (501)
pregnancies (501)
poverty (501)

About _____ of American adolescents begin having sexual intercourse between the ages of ____ and ____, and at least _____ have had intercourse by the time they are 20. This sexual activity, then, is beginning at a _____ age than in previous generations. The average boy first experiences intercourse at an _____ age than the average girl. One's _____, too, influences when one will begin having intercourse. Although the _____ standard has declined, it is still considered somewhat more permissible for _____ to be sexually active than for _____. The new standard, which is supplanting the old attitude, is permissiveness with _____.

While most adolescents are _____ and are sexually attracted to members of the opposite sex, a minority (between ___ and ___) are _____, attracted to members of their same sex. In addition, it is _____ for adolescents to have an isolated homosexual experience. Most researchers consider sexual orientation a _____, rather than seeing heterosexuality and homosexuality as polar opposites.

There is some data, generally based upon _____ samples, indicating a _____ or _____ basis for sexual orientation. Many psychologists favor an _____ explanation, but neither _____ theory nor _____ theory provides a satisfactory explanation. In any case, virtually all experts agree that sexual orientation is not a matter of _____. Homosexuality is _____ considered a psychological disorder, and although homosexual adolescents have higher _____ and _____ rates than heterosexual teens, in adulthood homosexuals have _____ degree of mental health as heterosexuals.

Every year 1 out of _____ American teenage girls becomes pregnant. Around _____ of teenage mothers are unmarried. Having a baby has ____ implications for a teenage mother's future. Teenage mothers frequently _____ of school and work in _____ jobs or go on _____. Their _____ may suffer due to the effects of stress.

The _____ born to adolescent mothers do not fare well, either. They are more likely to have _____ health and to perform poorly in _____. They are more likely to be involved in early _____ themselves and to be trapped in _____.

American teens are _____ likely to be involved in a pregnancy than teens in other industrialized countries, in spite of the fact that _____ rates are comparable. The difference is that American teens do not as regularly use _____. In addition, because American adults are basically _____ of premarital sex, our teens are less likely to receive _____ than teens in other industrialized countries.

more (501)

sexual activity (501)
birth control (501)
intolerant (501)
sex education (501)

_____ of Americans favor sex education for adolescents, but there is _____ agreement as to what should be taught. Teaching abstinence _____ proven effective. The best programs teach teens that they will personally _____ from avoiding pregnancy and also teach them how to _____ sexual advances. They teach them how to correctly use _____. These programs employ _____ and encourage _____ between parents and their children about sex. Finally, they educate adolescents as to the realities of _____.

90% (502)
little (502)
has not (502)
bencfit (503)

avert (503)
birth control (503); role-playing (503); discussions (503)
parenthood (503)

Crossword Puzzle

Social and Personality Development in Adolescence

Across

6 _____ delinquents usually begin misbehaving at an early age.

9 The joint influence of ethnicity and gender

10 _____ groups are those with whom one compares herself.

11 The psychosocial stage occurring during adolescence

12 The generation ____ is largely mythical.

13 _____ adolescents are ignored by their peers.

19 _____ adolescents are actively disliked by their peers.

20 Groups of 2-12 who have frequent social interaction with each other

21 Independence and a sense of control over one's life

22 James _____ expanded Erikson's views of identity formation.

23 _____ delinquents usually do not continue breaking the law as adults.

24 Many college students are in this identity state.

Down

1 _____ adolescents are those who are liked by some and disliked by others.

2 One who has made identity commitments without having undergone identity crises

3 Sexual attraction to members of one's own gender

4 Sexual self-stimulation

5 Identity _____: the state of having neither experienced crises or made commitments

7 Identity _____ results when one has had his or her crises and made his or her commitments.

8 Major _____ is a serious psychological disorder.

14 Sex _____ refers to the fact that adolescents spend most of their time in same-sex groups.

15 The _____ standard

16 Peer _____ leads to conformity.

17 _____ suicides occur when one suicide triggers others.

18 Social units larger than cliques

Flash Cards

Why do adolescents become more comfortable with their self-concepts towards the end of adolescence?	Contrast self-concept and self-esteem.
Why is girls' self-esteem lower than boys'?	Why do socioeconomic differences in self-esteem become more pronounced in later adolescence?
Name the three psychosocial stages that occur during adulthood.	Why does the identity search (usually) occur during adolescence?
Characterize someone who has achieved an identity.	Characterize someone who is an identity foreclosure.
Characterize someone who is identity diffused.	Characterize someone who is in a state of identity moratorium.

Having a self-concept is knowing yourself; self-esteem is liking yourself.	They come to accept that they are not totally consistent, and that different situations evoke different responses from them.
Because having possessions, such as a car, a good stereo, and nice clothes, become more salient at this time	Because girls are under more stress about their popularity, especially if they believe that academic success will undermine it
Because of cognitive and physical development; also, at this age individuals must begin to make choices that have life-long consequences	Intimacy vs. isolation; generativity vs stagnation; ego integrity vs despair
He or she has "always known" the course of their future and never had an identity crisis. They are rigid and need approval.	They had had both crises and commitments. They are mentally healthy and moral and achievement oriented.
These people are in the midst of their identity crises: they are seeking the best course for themselves and hence may be temporarily anxious.	Having neither experienced crises nor made commitments, these people are drifters who frequently change occupations and friends.

How common is adolescent depression?

Why are adolescent girls more likely to be depressed than adolescent boys?

How common are suicidal thoughts?

Why are adolescent boys more likely to commit suicide than adolescent girls?

List several warning signs of suicide.

What should you do if you suspect that someone you know is considering suicide?

Which types of societies tend to foster early adolescent attempts at autonomy? Which do not?

How big is the generation gap?

Why, according to Smetana, do adolescents and their parents disagree about many day-to-day behaviors?

Why do teens turn to peers for social comparisons and make them their reference group?

How does belonging to a certain crowd influence one's behavior?

How do cliques change over the course of adolescence?

Girls are under more stress due to role conflict, and they turn their stress inwards. Hormones do not appear to play a role in this gender difference.	Between 20% and 40% of adolescents have been depressed in the past six months, but only 3% will suffer from clinical levels of depression.
Although they make fewer attempts, they use more violent means and so are more often successful.	About 30% of teens have thought about suicide.
Talk to her, and ask about suicide. Seek professional help. Let her know you care. Collect the means. Get a commitment to postpone any action.	Making a will; talking about suicide; changes in personality; giving away possessions; preoccupation with death
It is quite small for important issues involving basic values and beliefs; it is more substantial for social and personal issues.	Individualistic societies (like the U.S.) promote early autonomy; collectivistic societies do not.
Because other teens have undergone similar experiences, they perceive their peers to be more similar to themselves than their parents.	Because parents view these behaviors as reflecting on values, whereas adolescents see them solely as matters of personal choice
At first they are unisex, then these unisex groups get together for parties. High-status members form new mixed-sex groups, which others then join.	Members of your crowd become your reference group and since you are identified with that crowd by others and by yourself, self-fulfilling prophecies develop.

Why does the clique system break up towards the end of high school?

Which late adolescents are most likely to have cross-racial friendships?

To whom do adolescents conform?

What are the warning signs that a child may develop into an undersocialized delinquent?

How does dating help teens?

Why are adolescents embarrassed about masturbation?

What is the "double standard?"

What is the most common adolescent attitude toward premarital sex?

Describe the data which suggests that there is a biological basis for sexual orientation.

Why might homosexual adolescents be more at risk of depression than heterosexual adolescents?

What does the future hold for most unwed teenage mothers?

Why are American teenage pregnancy rates so much higher than in other industrialized countries?

Those with extensive cross-racial experiences during childhood and those who attend schools that work to foster positive cross-racial interaction.

Adolescents' attention and efforts are directed towards dating and one-on-one cross-sex relationships.

Uncaring parents, school failure, peer rejection, low intelligence, early aggressive behavior, attention deficit disorder

To whomever they perceive an expert about a given issue. For social matters, these experts are usually peers; for basic values and future goals, parents.

They believe that only persons with no other sexual outlets masturbate. Also, society has traditionally had a negative view of this behavior.

It is fun, affects their status, and helps with identity formation. In late adolescence, it is a means of courtship and establishing emotional intimacy.

It is okay as long as you're in the midst of a long-term, loving, or committed relationship.

That, while it is OK for males to have sex, nice girls don't.

They are under much stress and are treated badly by others.

(1) The difference in concordance between fraternal and identical twins; (2) evidence of differences in brain structure; (3) evidence of hormonal differences.

American teenagers do not regularly use effective birth control.

Poverty. Even if not initially poor, most teenage mothers drop out of school and can get only very low-paying jobs.

How well do "Just Say No" programs work at decreasing adolescent pregnancy?

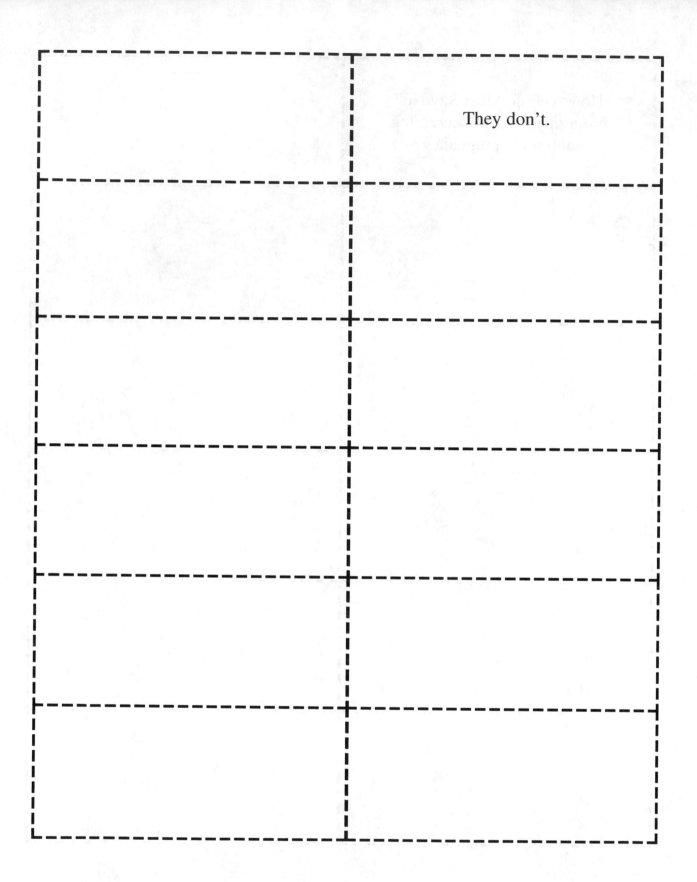

They don't.

Practice Test One

1. Adolescents are most comfortable with their self-concepts
   a. if they are female.
   b. during early adolescence.
   c. during middle adolescence.
   d. during late adolescence.

2. Who is apt to have the lowest self-esteem?
   a. Russell, a 16-year-old African-American male
   b. Helen, a 13-year-old Caucasian female
   c. Chip, an 18-year-old Caucasian male
   d. Ahna, a 14-year-old Asian-American female

3. Imelda has always known that she was going to be a dancer: her mother is a ballet instructor and she has been taking lessons since she was 3. She's never really considered doing anything else. Imelda is likely
   a. identity diffused.
   b. in a state of identity moratorium.
   c. a foreclosure.
   d. identity achieved.

4. The Brownly twins, Marsha and Ron, are both feeling very stressed because they are doing poorly in school. Which is the most likely outcome?
   a. Marsha will become depressed and Ron will impulsively pick a fight.
   b. Ron will become depressed and Marsha will impulsively pick a fight.
   c. Both Marsha and Ron will become depressed.
   d. Marsha will become hyperactive and Ron will socially withdraw.

5. Colleen has decided to commit suicide. Which method will she most likely use?
   a. a gun
   b. an overdose of sleeping pills
   c. crashing her car
   d. jumping from a window

6. Which should you avoid doing when confronting a friend who may be having suicidal thoughts?
   a. mention the possibility of suicide
   b. talk tough to them
   c. get a written commitment that they will delay taking any suicidal action
   d. finding a professional to help him or her

7. Parent-child conflict is most intense
   a. about basic values.
   b. during early adolescence.
   c. during late adolescence.
   d. between parents and their daughters.

8. Who provides the social norms for adolescents?
   a. their parents
   b. their friends
   c. their peers
   d. society at large

9. Cliques have at maximum about
    a. 4 members.
    b. 9 members.
    c. 12 members.
    d. 18 members.

10. By the end of high school, cliques
    a. are the dominant form of social interaction.
    b. are waning in importance.
    c. are mostly single-sex.
    d. only involve high-status individuals.

11. Which of the following helps account for the racial segregation that is seen even in desegre-gated high schools and colleges?
    a. negative attitudes
    b. differences in socioeconomic status
    c. differences in academic achievement levels
    d. all of the above

12. Controversial adolescents are most similar to
    a. popular adolescents.
    b. neglected adolescents.
    c. nonconformist adolescents.
    d. rejected adolescents.

13. Peter is a pretty typical 15-year old. For which problem will he turn to his father for advice?
    a. whether to dye his hair
    b. which Presidential candidate to support
    c. whether he should start smoking cigarettes
    d. none of the above

14. Seventeen-year-old Dmitri has a history of aggressive behavior and hence has few friends. He failed two grades in school and was held back for two years. At 13, he was diagnosed with attention-deficit disorder and last year was caught vandalizing a church. Which of the following is most likely true?
    a. He will engage in gang-based delinquent activities.
    b. He has over-protective parents.
    c. He will never be well-integrated into society.
    d. He will outgrow his criminal tendencies.

15. Dating in early or middle adolescence is least likely to involve
    a. sexual intimacy.
    b. psychological intimacy.
    c. fun and enjoyment.
    d. resolving identity issues.

16. Masturbation
    a. is considered acceptable by most teens.
    b. is a normal and harmless activity.
    c. can lead to physical weaknesses.
    d. is engaged in only if no sexual partner is available.

17. About _____ of American teens have experienced sexual intercourse by 20 years of age.
    a. 40%
    b. 50%
    c. 67%
    d. 80%

18. Which of the following statements about sexual orientation is true?
    a. People choose to be hetero- or homosexual.
    b. Learning theory does not adequately explain sexual orientation.
    c. There is most likely no biological basis for sexual orientation.
    d. Adolescents who have any homosexual experiences are likely to develop a homosexual orientation.

19. Which of the following statements about adolescent pregnancy is false?
    a. American teens are less likely to receive sex education than European teens.
    b. American teens are more sexually active than European teens.
    c. American teens are more likely to get pregnant than European teens.
    d. All of the above statements are false.

20. Which is the least successful sex education strategy?
    a. using role-playing
    b. teaching about the responsibilities of parenthood
    c. teaching only about abstinence
    d. teaching about effective contraception

Test Solutions

Self-Quiz Solution

1. d (page 477)
2. d (page 477)
3. c (page 480)
4. a (page 482)
5. b (page 483)
6. b (page 485)
7. b (page 487)
8. c (page 489)
9. c (page 490)
10. b (page 491)
11. d (page 492)
12. a (page 493)
13. b (page 494)
14. c (page 495)
15. b (page 497)
16. b (page 498)
17. d (page 498)
18. b (page 500)
19. b (page 500)
20. c (page 503)

Crossword Puzzle Solution

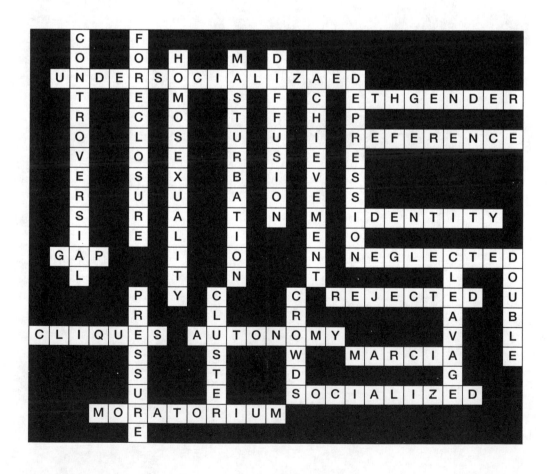